All-in-One Bible Fun

Heroes of the Bible

Preschool

Also available from Abingdon Press

All-in-One Bible Fun

Heroes of the Bible
Elementary

Fruit of the Spirit
Preschool

Fruit of the Spirit
Elementary

Stories of Jesus
Preschool

Stories of Jesus
Elementary

Favorite Bible Stories
Preschool

Favorite Bible Stories
Elementary

Writer/Editor: Daphna Flegal
Production Editors: Billie Brownell, Anna Raitt
Production and Design Manager: Marcia C'deBaca
Illustrator: Robert S. Jones
Cover images: jupiterimages

All-in-One

BIBLE

FUN

Heroes of the Bible
Preschool

ABINGDON PRESS
Nashville

All-in-One Bible Fun
Heroes of the Bible
Preschool

ISBN 9781426707841

Unless otherwise noted, Scripture quotations are from the New Revised Standard Version of the Bible, copyright © 1989, Division of Christian Education of the National Council of the Churches of Christ in the United States of America. Used by permission. All rights reserved.

Scripture quotations marked (GNT) are from the Good News Translation in Today's English Version - Second Edition © 1992 by American Bible Society. Used by Permission.

10 11 12 13 14 15 16 17 18 19 - 10 9 8 7 6 5 4 3 2 1

MANUFACTURED IN THE UNITED STATES OF AMERICA

All-in-One BIBLE FUN Table of Contents

Bible Units in *Heroes of the Bible*

Use these combinations if you choose to organize the lessons in short-term units.

Old Testament Heroes

Bible Story	Bible Verse
Daniel	Pray at all times. Romans 12:12, GNT
Jonah	Pray at all times. Romans 12:12, GNT
Joshua	Trust in the LORD. Psalm 37:3
Noah	Trust in the LORD. Psalm 37:3
David	I trust in God and am not afraid. Psalm 56:4, GNT
Miriam and Moses	Love one another. John 15:17
Esther	Love one another. John 15:17

New Testament Heroes

Bible Story	Bible Verse
Jesus and the Children	Let the children come to me. Luke 18:16, GNT
A Boy and His Lunch	Share what you have. Hebrew 13:16
Peter and John	Love is kind. 1 Corinthians 13:4
Dorcas	Love is kind. 1 Corinthians 13:4
Paul	Love is kind. 1 Corinthians 13:4
Lydia	Love is kind. 1 Corinthians 13:4

Supplies

(This is a comprehensive list of all the supplies needed if you choose to do all the activities. It is your choice whether your group will do all the activities.)

- Bible
- construction paper
- bulletin board border
- glue
- safety scissors, scissors
- clear tape
- masking tape
- stapler, staples
- crayons, markers
- ballpoint pen
- craft sticks
- newspaper
- paper bags, brown grocery bags
- napkins
- small paper plates
- animal crackers
- drinking straws
- paper punch
- ribbon or crepe paper

- doll, doll blanket
- scarfs or bandannas
- yarn or string
- ball
- beanbag
- towels or fabric, purple cloth
- chairs
- basket
- slice of bread or unsliced sandwich roll
- flashlight
- shallow pans
- Bible-times costume or shirt
- block, plastic bottle, or paper towel tube
- CD of Christian music and CD player
- 5-6 different items such as a box of crayons, book, toy, block, ball, or puzzle

 # Welcome to All-in-One Bible Fun

Have fun learning about heroes of the Bible! Each lesson in this teacher guide is filled with games and activities that will make learning fun for you and your children. Everything you need to teach is included in Abingdon's *All-in-One Bible Fun*, and with just a few additional supplies, your group can enjoy fun and enriching activities. Each lesson also has a box with a picture of a cookie,

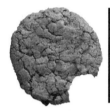

We can learn about Jesus.

that is repeated over and over again throughout the lesson. The cookie box states the Bible message in words your children will understand.

Use the following tips to help make *All-in-One Bible Fun* a success!

- Read through each lesson. Read the Bible passages.

- Memorize the Bible verse and the cookie box statement.

- Choose activities that fit your unique group of children and your time limitations. If time is limited, those activities we recommend are in **boldface** on the chart page and noted by a *balloon* beside each activity.

balloon symbol

- Practice telling the Bible story.

- Gather the supplies you will use for the lesson.

- Learn the music included in each lesson. All the songs are written to familiar tunes.

- Arrange your room space to fit the lesson. Move tables and chairs so there is plenty of room for the children to move and to sit on the floor.

- Copy the Reproducible pages for the lesson.

Preschoolers

Each child in your class is a one-of-a-kind child of God. Each child has his or her own name, background, family situation, and set of experiences. It is important to remember and celebrate the uniqueness of each child. Yet all of these one-of-a-kind children of God have some common needs.

- All children need love.
- All children need a sense of self-worth.
- All children need to feel a sense of accomplishment.
- All children need to have a safe place to be and to express their feelings.
- All children need to be surrounded by adults who love them.
- All children need to experience the love of God.

Preschoolers (children 3–5 years old) also have some common characteristics.

Their Bodies
- They do not sit still for very long.
- They have lots of energy.
- They enjoy moving (running, galloping, dancing, jumping, hopping).
- They are developing fine motor skills (learning to cut with scissors, learning to handle a ball, learning to tie their shoes).
- They enjoy using their senses (taste, touch, smell, hearing, seeing).

Their Minds
- They are learning more and more words.
- They enjoy music.
- They are learning to express their feelings.
- They like to laugh and be silly.
- They enjoy nonsense words.
- They are learning to identify colors, sizes, and shapes.
- They have an unclear understanding of time.
- They have a wonderful imagination.

Their Relationships
- They are beginning to interact with others as they play together.
- They are beginning to understand that other people have feelings.
- They are learning to wait for their turn.
- They can have a hard time leaving parents, especially their mother.
- They want to help.
- They love to feel important.

Their Hearts
- They need to handle the Bible and see others handle it.
- They need caring adults who model Christian attitudes and behaviors.
- They need to sing, move to, and say Bible verses.
- They need to hear clear, simple stories from the Bible.
- They can express simple prayers.
- They can experience wonder and awe at God's world.
- They can share food and money and make things for others.
- They can experience belonging at church.

All-in-One

BIBLE PRESCHOOL

FUN

Daniel

Bible Verse

Pray at all times.

Romans 12:12, GNT

Bible Story

Daniel 6:1-23, 25-28

The story of Daniel is a story of faith. The king was tricked into setting a law that said the people could pray only to him. If anyone broke this law, he or she would be put to death. Even though he knew the penalty for praying, Daniel remained faithful and continued praying to God. The people who tricked the king reported Daniel, and Daniel was put into a den of lions as punishment. God delivered Daniel, and the king made a new law telling all the people to honor God.

Daniel was taken captive as a young man and brought to Babylon with other captives. He was selected by the king to be trained for service at court. This meant that he was educated in many of the important subjects of the time. He was probably taught reading, writing, mathematics, medicine, and astronomy. Even though Daniel was educated by the king, he remained faithful to God.

As Daniel matured, he became a successful and trusted official in the court. His faith in

God was the reason behind Daniel's success. At the time of the story with the lions, he held an important position for the king. Some of the other officials for the king became jealous of Daniel's success. They plotted to get rid of Daniel by tricking the king and using Daniel's faithfulness against him. The plot backfired, however, as God intervened and delivered Daniel.

Daniel must have been afraid when he faced the den of lions. Yet he kept his trust in God. For Daniel, prayer became a tool for trusting God.

Young children experience all of life's emotions, from happiness to fear. As teachers and parents we can help children learn to pray for God's help in all situations and at all times. Modeling prayer as an everyday habit in our own lives is an effective way to help children learn to ask for God's help. Take a few moments and pray for your children right now.

We can talk to God and ask God to help us.

If time is limited, we recommend those activities that are noted in **boldface**. Depending on your time and the number of children, you may be able to include more activities.

ACTIVITY	TIME	SUPPLIES
Lion Lineup	5 minutes	Reproducible 1A, construction paper, scissors
Face a Lion	**10 minutes**	**Reproducible 1A, small paper plates, safety scissors, crayons, craft sticks, glue, masking tape**
Rainbow Romp	5 minutes	lion puppets from "Face a Lion" activity (Reproducible 1A), different colors of ribbons or crepe paper streamers, scissors, tape
Bible Story: Daniel and the Lions	**10 minutes**	**lion puppets (Reproducible 1A), scarf or bandanna**
Bible Verse Fun	**5 minutes**	**Bible, lion puppets (Reproducible 1A)**
Sleep, Lion, Sleep	5 minutes	None
Leaping Lions	10 minutes	Reproducible 1A, scissors, masking tape
Face Freeze	5 minutes	Reproducible 1B, scissors
Roll a Prayer	**5 minutes**	**ball**

JOIN THE FUN

BIBLE STORY FUN

LIVE THE FUN

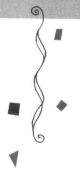

Lion Lineup

Photocopy the lion faces and lion pictures **(Reproducible 1A)**. Make enough copies for each child plus one more. Cut the lion faces and lion pictures apart along the solid line. Use the lion faces in the "Face a Lion" activity.

Place one lion picture on a table or on the rug. Cut the construction paper into one-inch strips. Cover the lion picture with the strips. As the children arrive for today's lesson, show the children the covered picture. Take away one strip of paper.

Ask: Can you tell me what this picture is?

Continue to remove strips of paper one at a time until the children guess that the picture is of a lion.

Say: Today our Bible story is about a man named Daniel. Daniel had to spend the night with lions. Daniel was afraid, so he talked to God and asked God to help him. We can talk to God and ask God to help us when we feel afraid. We can talk to God anytime.

We can talk to God and ask God to help us.

Face a Lion

Photocopy the lion faces and lion pictures **(Reproducible 1A)** if you haven't already. Give each child a lion picture. Let the children color the lions with crayons. Write each child's name on his or her picture. Print each name in large letters. Line the lion pictures up in your story area.

Cut out a lion face **(Reproducible 1A)** for each child. Let the children color the lion faces with crayons. Give each child a small paper plate. Have the child glue the lion face in the middle of the paper plate.

Give each child a pair of safety scissors. Show the children how to use the scissors to make cuts around the edge of the paper plate. This will make the lions' manes. Remember that young children are learning to use scissors. They need to practice their cutting skills. Affirm their efforts.

Glue or tape the paper plates onto craft sticks to make puppets.

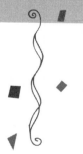

Rainbow Romp

Cut several different colors of ribbons or crepe paper streamers into 12-inch lengths. Gather all the ribbons or streamers together. Wrap tape around one of the ends to make a rainbow streamer. Wave the rainbow streamer as you lead the children around the room to your story area. Let the children hold their lion puppets from "Face a Lion" activity **(Reproducible 1A).**

Supplies

lion puppets from "Face a Lion" activity (Reproducible 1A), different colors of ribbons or crepe paper streamers, scissors, tape

Come, follow me on a rainbow
   romp.
We'll step, step, step and
   stomp, stomp, stomp.
(Wave the rainbow streamer.)

Let's step, step, step,
Step, step, step to our story.
(Step around the room.)

Come, follow me on a rainbow
   romp.
We'll step, step, step and
   stomp, stomp, stomp.
(Wave the rainbow streamer.)

Let's stomp, stomp, stomp,
Stomp, stomp, stomp to our story.
(Stomp around the room.)

Come, follow me on a rainbow
   romp.
We'll step, step, step and
   stomp, stomp, stomp.
(Wave the rainbow streamer.)

Let's roar, roar, roar,
Roar, roar, roar to our story.
*(Have children hold up lion puppets
and roar.)*

Come, follow me on a rainbow
   romp.
We'll step, step, step and
   stomp, stomp, stomp.
(Wave the rainbow streamer.)

(Quiet voice.)
Let's tip, tip, toe,
Tip, tip, toe to our story.
(Walk on tiptoes.)

(Continue to speak in a quiet voice.)
Come, follow me on a rainbow
   romp.
We'll step, step, step and
   stomp, stomp, stomp.
(Wave the rainbow streamer.)

(Whisper.)
Let's sit, sit, sit,
Sit, sit, sit for our story.
*(Have children sit down in your story
area.)*

Say: Today our Bible story is about a man named Daniel and the lions.

We can talk to God and ask God to help us.

Daniel and the Lions

by Daphna Flegal

Play a game with the children before telling the story. Have the children hold up their lion face puppets (**Reproducible 1A**) *and roar like lions. Show the children a scarf or bandanna.*

Say: Watch as I throw the scarf into the air. As long as the scarf is in the air, hold up your lion faces and roar like lions. When the scarf touches the floor, you must stop roaring.

Throw the scarf into the air and encourage the children to roar like lions. Have the children stop making sounds when the scarf touches the floor. Throw the scarf two or three times.

Say: Our Bible story today tells us about Daniel and the lions. Whenever I say *lions,* **I will throw the scarf in the air. Hold up your lion faces and roar until the scarf touches the floor. Stop roaring when the scarf touches the floor.**

Tell the story, throwing the scarf each time you say the word "lions." After the scarf touches the floor, pick up the scarf and continue the story.

Daniel loved God. He prayed to God every day. Daniel was the king's helper. He worked very hard for the king. But there were some men who did not like Daniel. They wanted Daniel's job as the king's helper. These men tried to make trouble for Daniel. They wanted to throw Daniel to some very hungry **lions**.

They tricked the king into making a new rule. The new rule said that everyone had to pray to the king, not to God. If someone did not pray to the king, he or she had to go in with the **lions**.

"The king is my friend," said Daniel. "But I cannot pray to the king. I pray to God."

The men watched Daniel pray to God. Then they ran to the king. "Daniel has broken your new rule," said the men. "Now you must throw him to the **lions**."

The king was very sad. But the king had to obey the new rule. "I pray that your God

will take care of you, Daniel," said the king. He put Daniel in with the **lions**.

The king worried all night. He kept thinking about Daniel and the **lions**.

The next morning the king hurried to Daniel. "Daniel, Daniel," cried the king. "Are you all right?"

"Yes, answered Daniel. "I'm fine. I prayed to God and asked God to help me." Daniel walked out of the **lion's** den.

"I'm happy your God kept you safe," said the king. "Now I will make a new rule. Everyone will pray to your God."

Daniel continued to pray to God every day. He knew he could talk to God and ask God to help him anytime.

Bible Verse Fun

Choose a child to hold the Bible open to Romans 12:12.

Say: Daniel prayed to God. He talked to God and asked God to help him.

> ## We can talk to God and ask God to help us.

Say the Bible verse, "Pray at all times" (Romans 12:12, GNT), for the children. Have the children repeat the Bible verse after you.

Help the children learn the Bible verse by singing. Sing the words printed below to the tune of "God Is So Good."

"Pray at all times."
"Pray at all times."
"Pray at all times."
Is our Bible verse.

Let the children sing a song about the Bible story. Have the children hold their lion puppets **(Reproducible 1A)**. Sing the song printed below to the tune of "The Farmer In the Dell."

Daniel

O Daniel prayed to God,
O Daniel prayed to God.
They threw him in the lion's den
because he prayed to God.
(Hold up the lion puppets.)

But God kept Daniel safe,
but God kept Daniel safe.
Even in the lion's den
(Hold up the lion puppets.)
his God kept Daniel safe.

Words: Daphna Flegal and Sharilyn S. Adair
© 1997 Abingdon Press

Supplies

None

Sleep, Lion, Sleep

Have the children move to an open area of the room. Tell the children to pretend that you are Daniel. Encourage the children to pretend to be lions. Let them get on their hands and knees, crawl around Daniel, and roar. Walk to each lion, pat the lion on the head, and say, "Sleep, lion, sleep." Each lion should then curl up on the floor as if sleeping. After all the lions are asleep, play the game again and let a child pretend to be Daniel.

Supplies

Reproducible 1A, scissors, masking tape

Leaping Lions

Use the lion pictures **(Reproducible 1A)** from the "Lion Lineup" (see page 12). Make sure each lion picture has a child's name written on it. If the pictures are lined up in your story area, have each child find the lion with her or his name printed on it. Help any children who cannot identify their names to find their pictures.

If you did not use the lion pictures in the "Lion Lineup," give each child a lion picture now. Write each child's name on his or her picture.

Make a long straight line on the floor with masking tape. Tape the lion pictures along the line. Have the children start at the beginning of the line. Choose one child to begin.

Say: Leap to lion (*child's name*).

Have the child leap (make several short jumps) from the beginning of the line to the lion with his or her name. Have the child stand still on the lion.

Say: (*Child's name*), **"Pray at all times"** (Romans 12:12, GNT).

Encourage the child to repeat the Bible verse. Continue with the next child. Change the directions to vary the movements: **"Hop** (*jump, tiptoe, march*) **to lion** (*child's name*).**"**

Say: Our Bible verse helps us remember that:

We can talk to God and ask God to help us.

Face Freeze

Supplies

Reproducible
1B, scissors

Photocopy the faces **(Reproducible 1B)**. Cut the faces apart along the solid lines. Have the children sit in a circle. Show the children the faces one at a time. Help the children identify the feelings represented by each of the faces.

Ask: What makes you happy? sad? afraid? mad?

Say: In our Bible story Daniel was afraid of the lions. When Daniel was afraid, he prayed to God. He talked to God and asked God to help him.

> ## We can talk to God and ask God to help us.

Mix up the face pictures. Choose one of the pictures and show it to the child sitting next to you in the circle. Tell that child to make a face like the one in the picture. Tell the child to "freeze"\" his or her face. Have the child show his or her face (with the "frozen" expression) to the next child. The next child freezes her or his face in the same way and then turns to the child next in the circle. Give each child a turn to freeze their face and turn to the next child.

Say: We can talk to God and ask God to help us when we are (*name whatever feeling the face picture represents*).

Repeat the game with the remaining pictures.

Roll a Prayer

Supplies

ball

Have the children sit in a circle with their legs spread out in front of them.

Say: We can talk to God anytime. We can talk to God and ask God to help us. Let's talk to God right now.

Roll the ball to a child.

Say: Thank you, God, for (*child's name*). **Amen.**

Have the child roll the ball back to you. Repeat with each child in the circle.

REPRODUCIBLE 1A

Happy

Sad

Afraid

Mad

Heroes of the Bible - Preschool

All-in-One
BIBLE PRESCHOOL
FUN

Jonah

Bible Verse

Pray at all times.

Romans 12:12, GNT

Bible Story

Jonah 1–2:1-2, 10; 3:1-3

God called Jonah to go to Ninevah. Jonah tried to run away from God by taking a ship to Tarshish. God caused a storm at sea, and Jonah acknowledged that he was the cause of the storm. He allowed himself to be thrown overboard and wound up in the belly of a great fish. Jonah prayed to God, and the fish spit him out onto dry land. God again told Jonah to go to Ninevah. This time, Jonah agreed to go.

God refused to give up on Jonah even when Jonah tried to run away. God used the fish to save Jonah; it represents God's grace. When Jonah prayed, God responded, and Jonah finally fulfilled his mission.

The fish can make this story appealing to young children. The fish also can make this story scary. Be careful how you present the story. Emphasize God's love for Jonah and how the fish helped Jonah know that he could pray to God anywhere and anytime.

When talking about prayer with young children, help them understand that prayer is simply talking and listening to God. Pray with your children sometime during every class time. Pray for the children by name. Take time to pray for any of the children's family members who may be ill.

Use structured prayers with your children. The children can learn simple prayers to use at snack time or in worship time.

Also encourage the use of spontaneous prayers with the children. Say prayers in the midst of activities. For example, you might pray, "Thank you, God, for friends to play with. Amen." when the children are playing well together. Or, "Thank you, God, for rain that helps the flowers grow. Amen." during class time on a rainy day. These kinds of spontaneous prayers will help your children understand that we can "pray at all times" (Romans 12:12, GNT).

We can talk to God anywhere and anytime.

If time is limited, we recommend those activities that are noted in **boldface**. Depending on your time and the number of children, you may be able to include more activities.

ACTIVITY	TIME	SUPPLIES
Fish Fun	**10 minutes**	**Reproducible 2A, scissors**
Fish Walk	10 minutes	Reproducible 2A, scissors, masking tape, optional: CD of Christian music and CD player
Rainbow Romp	5 minutes	different colors of ribbons or crepe paper streamers, scissors, tape
Bible Story: Go, Jonah, Go!	**10 minutes**	**None**
Bible Verse Fun	**5 minutes**	**Bible**
An Echo Fish Story	10 minutes	None
Jonah-in-the-Fish	5 minutes	None
Prayer Fish	10 minutes	Reproducible 2B, scissors, crayons, or markers
Roll a Prayer	**5 minutes**	**ball**

JOIN THE FUN

BIBLE STORY FUN

LIVE THE FUN

Fish Fun

Photocopy the fish cards (**Reproducible 2A**). You will need at least two sets of the cards for "Fish Fun." Cut the cards apart. Place the sets of fish cards on a table or on the rug.

Say: Today our Bible story is about a man named Jonah and a big fish. The fish helped Jonah learn that we can talk to God anywhere and anytime. When we talk to God, we are praying to God.

Ask: When do you pray? *(at meals, before bedtime, at Sunday school)*

We can pray to God anywhere and anytime.

Say: Jonah prayed to God when he was inside the belly of a big fish! Find a card that shows Jonah inside the fish. Now find the card that matches.

Let the children enjoy matching the cards.

Fish Walk

Photocopy and cut apart the fish cards (**Reproducible 2A**). You will need as many cards as you have children. Have a variety of cards showing Jonah in different positions. Place the fish cards on the floor in a circle. Secure the cards to the floor with masking tape. Show the children the fish cards.

Say: Today our Bible story is about a man named Jonah and a big fish. The fish helped Jonah know that he could talk to God anywhere and anytime.

Have the children walk around the circle of fish cards as you sing the Bible verse song (see page 23). Stop singing. Have each child stand on a fish card. Instruct the children to look at their cards.

Ask: What is Jonah doing inside the fish?

Have the children move their bodies to copy the motion Jonah is doing on the fish cards. Continue the game as the children show interest. If you are uncomfortable singing, use music from a Christian CD.

Say: Jonah prayed to God when he was inside the fish. We can pray to God anywhere we are.

Rainbow Romp

Supplies

different colors of ribbons or crepe paper streamers, scissors, tape

Cut several different colors of ribbons or crepe paper streamers into 12-inch lengths. Gather all the ribbons or streamers together. Wrap tape around one of the ends to make a rainbow streamer. Wave the rainbow streamer as you lead the children around the room to your story area.

Come, follow me on a rainbow romp.
We'll step, step, step and stomp, stomp, stomp.
(Wave the rainbow streamer.)

Let's step, step, step,
Step, step, step to our story.
(Step around the room.)

Come, follow me on a rainbow romp.
We'll step, step, step and stomp, stomp, stomp.
(Wave the rainbow streamer.)

Let's stomp, stomp, stomp,
Stomp, stomp, stomp to our story.
(Stomp around the room.)

Come, follow me on a rainbow romp.
We'll step, step, step and stomp, stomp, stomp.
(Wave the rainbow streamer.)

Let's swim, swim, swim,
Swim, swim, swim to our story.
(Pretend to swim around the room.)

Come, follow me on a rainbow romp.
We'll step, step, step and stomp, stomp, stomp.
(Wave the rainbow streamer.)

(Speak in a quiet voice.)
Let's tip, tip, toe,
Tip, tip, toe to our story.
(Walk on tiptoes.)

(Continue to speak in a quiet voice.)
Come, follow me on a rainbow romp.
We'll step, step, step and stomp, stomp, stomp.
(Wave the rainbow streamer.)

(Whisper.)
Let's sit, sit, sit,
Sit, sit, sit for our story.
(Have the children sit down in your story area.)

Say: Today our Bible story is about a man named Jonah and a big fish. The fish helped Jonah know he could pray to God anywhere and anytime.

We can pray to God anywhere and anytime.

Go, Jonah, Go!

by Daphna Flegal

Have the children raise their arms in the air, shake their fists, and say, **"Go, Jonah, go! Go, go, go!"** *each time you say,* **God said, "Go, go, go!"**

"Jonah," God said, "go to Ninevah and tell the people about my love." **God said, "Go, go, go!"**

Go, Jonah, go!
Go, go, go!
(Raise arms in the air and shake fists.)

"No," Jonah said to God. "I don't want to go to Ninevah." But **God said, "Go, go, go!"**

Go, Jonah, go!
Go, go, go!
(Raise arms in the air and shake fists.)

"I'm going to run away," said Jonah. "I will go someplace where God cannot find me." He got on a boat and sailed to a place far away from Ninevah. But **God said, "Go, go, go!"**

Go, Jonah, go!
Go, go, go!
(Raise arms in the air and shake fists.)

When Jonah got onto the boat, he went to sleep. While Jonah was sleeping, the wind began to blow. Waves tossed the boat back and forth, back and forth. Everyone on the boat was afraid. But **God said, "Go, go, go!"**

Go, Jonah, go!
Go, go, go!
(Raise arms in the air and shake fists.)

"Wake up, wake up," the others on the boat called to Jonah. "Wake up and pray with us." Jonah woke up.

"God sent this storm," said Jonah, "because I tried to run away from God. If you want to stop the storm, throw me into the water." And **God said, "Go, go, go!"**

Go, Jonah, go!
Go, go, go!
(Raise arms in the air and shake fists.)

The others picked Jonah up and threw him into the water. The wind stopped blowing. The waves stopped rocking the boat back and forth. God sent a fish to swallow Jonah to keep him safe in the water. And **God said, "Go, go, go!"**

Go, Jonah, go!
Go, go, go!
(Raise arms in the air and shake fists.)

Jonah prayed to God from inside the fish. "I will not try to run away from you again," Jonah said to God. "I will go to Ninevah and tell the people about your love."

The fish spit Jonah onto dry land. Jonah went to Ninevah because **God said, "Go, go, go!"**

Go, Jonah, go!
Go, go, go!
(Raise arms in the air and shake fists.)

Bible Verse Fun

Choose a child to hold the Bible open to Romans 12:12.

Say: Jonah prayed to God when he was inside the fish. God heard Jonah's prayer.

> ## We can pray to God anywhere and anytime.

Say the Bible verse, "Pray at all times" (Romans 12:12, GNT), for the children. Have the children repeat the Bible verse after you.

Help the children learn the Bible verse by singing. Sing the words printed below to the tune of "God Is So Good."

> "Pray at all times."
> "Pray at all times."
> "Pray at all times."
> Is our Bible verse.

Sing the song printed below to the tune of "The Farmer in the Dell."

Anywhere and Anytime

Oh, Jonah prayed to God.
(Fold hands in prayer.)
Oh, Jonah prayed to God.
(Fold hands in prayer.)
From the belly of a fish,
(Rub stomach; move hands like fins.)
Oh, Jonah prayed to God.
(Fold hands in prayer.)

Oh, we can pray to God.
(Fold hands in prayer.)
Oh, we can pray to God.
(Fold hands in prayer.)
Anywhere and anytime,
*(Hold out arms and turn around;
pretend to tap your wristwatch.)*
Oh, we can pray to God.
(Fold hands in prayer.)

An Echo Fish Story

Enjoy using the echo story with your children. Encourage the children to say what you say and to do what you do.

"Jonah, Jonah," said God one day, *(Shake your index finger.)*
"Go to Ninevah, go right away!" *(Point far away.)*

"No, no, no," Jonah answered that day, *(Put hands on legs.)*
"I won't go to Ninevah. I'll run away." *(Pat hands on legs.)*

So Jonah took a ride on a great big boat, *(Rock back and forth.)*
And went to sleep while he was afloat. *(Place hands under cheek as if sleeping.)*

Then the wind started blowing and the waves crashed about. *(Rock.)*
"Wake up, Jonah," the men began to shout. *(Cup hands around mouth.)*

Jonah woke up and saw the ocean waves. *(Put hand over eyes.)*
"Throw me in the water so that you can be saved." *(Pretend to dive into the water.)*

The men picked up Jonah and threw him in the sea. *(Pretend to swim.)*
Where a great big fish just happened to be. *(Put palms together to make fish movements with your hands.)*

The fish swallowed Jonah down into its belly. *(Rub stomach.)*
He stayed there three days all wet and smelly. *(Pinch nose.)*

While inside the fish Jonah prayed and prayed. *(Fold hands in prayer.)*
God heard his prayers from where they were made. *(Cup ears.)*

The fish spit Jonah out onto dry land. *(Make fish movements with your hands. Open palms and then snap them back together.)*
Then Jonah went to Ninevah, just as God planned. *(Walk in place.)*

Jonah-in-the-Fish

Say: Jonah was swallowed by a great big fish. Let's pretend to be Jonah sitting in the fish.

Have the children fold their hands as if praying and crouch down while you say the first three lines of the rhyme. On the last line have the children jump up and say, "Yes, I will!"

**Jonah-in-the-fish,
Sitting so still,
Won't you go to Ninevah?
Yes, I will!**

Prayer Fish

Photocopy the prayer fish **(Reproducible 2B)** for each child. Let the children decorate the fish with crayons or markers. As the children are working, talk with them about prayer.

Say: Jonah prayed to God from inside the fish. We can pray to God anywhere and anytime. When do you pray? *(At meals, before bedtime.)* **Can you pray when you are riding in the car?** *(Yes.)* **Can you pray when you are playing with toys?** *(Yes.)* **When you are sad?** *(Yes.)* **When you are happy?** *(Yes.)*

Have the children hold up their prayer fish.

Say: Your fish can help you remember that you can talk to God anywhere and anytime.

Read the Bible verse printed on the fish to the children. Have the children repeat the verse.

Say the following rhyme for the children. Have the children hold up their fish on the last line.

> **We can say a prayer to God**
> **Anywhere we wish.**
> **We can say a prayer to God,**
> **Even from a fish!**
> *(Hold up fish.)*

Roll a Prayer

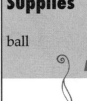

Have the children sit in a circle with their legs spread out in front of them.

Say: We can talk to God anytime. We can talk to God and ask God to help us. Let's talk to God right now.

Roll the ball to a child.

Say: Thank you, God, for *(child's name).* **Amen.**

Have the child roll the ball back to you. Repeat with each child in the circle.

Supplies

Reproducible 2B, crayons or markers

Supplies

ball

REPRODUCIBLE 2A

ALL–IN–ONE BIBLE FUN

REPRODUCIBLE 2B

All-in-One

BIBLE PRESCHOOL

FUN

Joshua

Bible Verse

Trust in the LORD.

Psalm 37:3

Bible Story

Joshua 6:1-16, 20

Joshua and the battle of Jericho is the story of how the Hebrew people captured the walled city of Jericho. The story is incredible. Joshua and the people marched around the wall one time every day for six days. Each day the people marched in silence. On the seventh day the seven priests leading the people blew on trumpets. At the sound of the trumpets the people who had marched so silently each day shouted with a great shout—and the walls fell down!

This story is the continuation of the Hebrew people's exodus from Egypt. The people had escaped from Egypt and had lived in the wilderness for forty years. Moses was dead, and Joshua was their new leader. God had promised the Hebrew people that they would live in the promised land. That land, however, was already occupied by other people.

The land God promised the Hebrew people was the land of Canaan. Jericho was an im-portant city in Canaan because it guarded the entrance to the valley. The people had to conquer Jericho in order to enter Canaan. But the city of Jericho was surrounded by a wall. God gave Joshua very clear directions on what to do in order to take Jericho. When Joshua and the people did what God commanded, the walls fell flat, and Jericho was delivered into the hands of the Hebrews.

Knowing what God wants us to do is not always as clear as God's directions to Joshua. But the Bible can help us discern what God wants us to do. The Bible tells us it is important to love God and to love one another (Matthew 22:37-39). The Bible tells us to praise God (Psalm 150). The Bible also tells us to be kind to one another (Ephesians 4:32), to share with one another (Acts 4:32), and to pray (Romans 12:12). We can help young children begin to know what God wants them to do in their lives by introducing them to these Biblical teachings.

We can trust God and do what God wants us to do.

If time is limited, we recommend those activities that are noted in **boldface**. Depending on your time and the number of children, you may be able to include more activities.

ACTIVITY	TIME	SUPPLIES	
This Way to Jericho	10 minutes	paper bags, newspaper, masking tape	**JOIN THE FUN**
Trumpet Tunes	**10 minutes**	**Reproducible 3A, crayons, clear tape**	
Rainbow Romp	5 minutes	trumpets (Reproducible 3A), different colors of ribbons or crepe paper streamers, scissors, tape	**BIBLE STORY FUN**
Bible Story: The Great Big Wall	**10 minutes**	**trumpets (Reproducible 3A)**	
Bible Verse Fun	**5 minutes**	**Bible**	
Jericho Jump	10 minutes	paper bags, newspaper, masking tape	
Ring 'Round Jericho	5 minutes	paper bags, newspaper, masking tape	
Trust and Do Circle	5 minutes	Reproducible 3B, paper bag	**LIVE THE FUN**
Roll a Prayer	**5 minutes**	**ball**	

paper bags,
newspaper,
masking tape

This Way to Jericho

Set out paper bags and newspapers on the table or floor. Show the children how to crumple sheets of newspaper and stuff them inside the bags. Fold over the top of the bags and seal the bags shut with masking tape.

Say: Today's Bible story is about a man named Joshua. God told Joshua to take the people into a city called Jericho, but there was a big wall all around the city of Jericho. Joshua could not take the people into Jericho because of the wall.

Show the children how to stack the bags to build a wall.

Say: Let's pretend that our paper bags are stones. Let's use the stones to build the wall around Jericho.

Make sure that the children build the wall so that there is space to march around the wall.

Reproducible
3A, crayons,
clear tape

Trumpet Tunes

Photocopy the paper horns (**Reproducible 3A**) for each child. Let the children decorate the paper horns with crayons. Help the children roll their papers into a horn shape. Tape the edges together. Show the children how to hold their horns up to their mouths and pretend to blow.

Say: God wanted Joshua to take the people into the city of Jericho, but there was a big wall around the city to keep Joshua and the people out. God told Joshua to have the people march around the walls. Seven men led the people around the walls. The men blew on trumpets as they marched. Joshua trusted God and did what God wanted him to do.

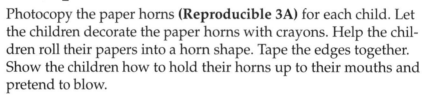

We can trust God and do what God wants us to do.

Have the children hold their trumpets and follow you in the "Rainbow Romp" activity.

Rainbow Romp

Cut several different colors of ribbons or crepe paper streamers into 12-inch lengths. Gather all the ribbons or streamers together. Wrap tape around one of the ends to make a rainbow streamer.

Have the children hold their paper trumpets **(Reproducible 3A)** and follow you as you wave the rainbow streamer and lead the children around the wall and then to your story area.

Supplies

trumpets (Reproducible 3A), different colors of ribbons or crepe paper streamers, scissors, tape

Come, follow me on a rainbow romp.
We'll step, step, step and stomp, stomp, stomp.
(Wave the rainbow streamer.)

Let's step, step, step,
Step, step, step to our story.
(Step around the room.)

Come, follow me on a rainbow romp.
We'll step, step, step and stomp, stomp, stomp.
(Wave the rainbow streamer.)

Let's stomp, stomp, stomp,
Stomp, stomp, stomp to our story.
(Stomp around the room.)

Come, follow me on a rainbow romp.
We'll step, step, step and stomp, stomp, stomp.
(Wave the rainbow streamer.)

Let's march, march, march,
March, march, march to our story.
(Pretend to blow the trumpets; march around the room.)

Come, follow me on a rainbow romp.
We'll step, step, step and stomp, stomp, stomp.
(Wave the rainbow streamer.)

(Speak in a quiet voice.)
Let's tip, tip, toe,
Tip, tip, toe to our story.
(Walk on tiptoes.)

(Continue to speak in a quiet voice.)
Come, follow me on a rainbow romp.
We'll step, step, step and stomp, stomp, stomp.
(Wave the rainbow streamer.)

(Whisper.)
Let's sit, sit, sit,
Sit, sit, sit for our story.
(Have the children sit down in your story area.)

Say: Our Bible story is about a man named Joshua. God told Joshua to take the people into the city of Jericho. Joshua trusted God.

The Great Big Wall

by Daphna Flegal

*Have the children place their paper trumpets (**Reproducible 3A**) behind them or under their chairs.*

"The city of Jericho will be your new home," God told Joshua.

"How can I take the people to live in the city of Jericho?" Joshua asked. "There is a great big wall all around the city."

"Have the people march around the wall," said God.

Joshua trusted God and did what God told him to do.

The city of Jericho
(Hold arms up above head with tips of fingers touching to make a rooftop.)
Has a great big wall.
(Hold arms out straight at shoulder height.)
Can't go over it.
(Shake head no.)
Can't go under it.
(Shake head no.)
Let's march around it.
(Pat legs.)

"March around the wall every day for six days," said God.

Joshua trusted God and did what God told him to do.

The city of Jericho
(Hold arms up above head with tips of fingers touching to make a rooftop.)
Has a great big wall.
(Hold arms out straight at shoulder height.)
Can't go over it.
(Shake head no.)
Can't go under it.
(Shake head no.)
Let's march around it.
(Pat legs.)

"Now march around the wall seven times," said God. "Have the priests blow on their trumpets. As soon as you hear the trumpet sounds, have all the people shout."

Joshua trusted God and did what God told him to do.

The city of Jericho
(Hold arms up above head with tips of fingers touching to make a rooftop.)
Has a great big wall.
(Hold arms out straight at shoulder height.)
Can't go over it.
(Shake head no.)
Can't go under it.
(Shake head no.)
Let's march around it.
(Pat legs.)
Hear the trumpets blow!
(Hold up paper horns and pretend to blow. Then put horns on floor.)

When the people heard the trumpets, they began to shout. The great big wall began to tremble. The stones began to crack. Then the great big wall FELL DOWN!

The city of Jericho
(Hold arms up above head with tips of fingers touching to make a rooftop.)
Has a great big wall.
(Hold arms out straight at shoulder height.)
Can't go under it.
(Shake head no.)
But we can go over it.
(Shake head yes.)
'Cause the great big wall fell down!
(Quickly drop arms to sides.)

Joshua and the people went over the crumbled wall and made their home in the city of Jericho. Joshua trusted God and did what God told him to do.

Bible Verse Fun

Choose a child to hold the Bible open to Psalm 37:3.

Say: Joshua trusted God and did what God wanted him to do.

> ## We can trust God and do what God wants us to do.

Say the Bible verse, "Trust in the LORD" (Psalm 37:3), for the children. Have the children repeat the Bible verse after you.

Help the children learn the Bible verse by singing. Sing the words printed below to the tune of "Do You Know the Muffin Man?"

> We can say the Bible verse,
> the Bible verse, the Bible verse.
> We can say the Bible verse,
> It's "Trust in the LORD."

Have the children stand in a circle in an open area of the room. Sing the song printed below and do the suggested motions. The tune is "This the Way."

All Around the City

This the way we march around,
(March around the circle.)
March around, march around.
This is the way we march around,
All around the city.

This the way we blow our horns,
(Cup hands around mouth.)
Blow our horns, blow our horns.
This the way we blow our horns,
All around the city.

This the way we shout and yell,
(Shake fists in the air.)
Shout and yell, shout and yell.
This the way we shout and yell,
All around the city.

This the way the walls fall down,
(Bring hands over head; shake hands and bring them down to the floor.)
Walls fall down, walls fall down.
This the way the walls fall down,
All around the city.

Words: Daphna Flegal
© 2001 Abingdon Press

Supplies

paper bags,
newspaper,
masking tape

Jericho Jump

If you did the "This Way to Jericho" activity, take four of the paper bag stones from the pretend wall (see page 32). Set the four bags in a line with space between each bag.

Let the children take turns jumping over the four paper bag stones. As each child jumps over each bag, have the child say one word of the Bible verse, Psalm 37:3: Trust *(Jump over first bag.)* in *(Jump over second bag.)* the *(Jump over third bag.)* LORD. *(Jump over fourth bag.)*

Say: Joshua trusted God and did what God wanted him to do. We can trust God and do what God wants us to do.

We can trust God and do what God wants us to do.

Supplies

paper bags,
newspaper,
masking tape

Ring 'Round Jericho

Build a paper bag wall or replace the four paper bag stones in the wall (see page 32). Have the children stand in a circle around the paper bag wall and hold hands. Lead the children around the circle as you recite this rhyme:

> **One time around the city walls,**
> **They marched round and round.**
> **One time around the city walls.**
> **Will the walls come falling down?**

Have the children stop walking on the last line. Repeat the verse and have the children walk in a circle again. Change the number in the rhyme (two, three, four, five, six). On the seventh time use the next stanza of the rhyme and let the children knock down the paper bag wall. If you chose not to build the paper wall, let the children fall down on the floor as in "Ring Around the Rosy."

> **Seven times around the city walls,**
> **They marched round and round.**
> **Seven times around the city walls.**
> **See the walls come falling down!**

If you prefer to play the game twice instead of seven times, begin with "Six times around the city walls" instead of "One time around the city walls."

Say: God told Joshua to march with the people around the walls of Jericho. Joshua trusted God and did what God wanted him to do.

Trust and Do Circle

Photocopy the Trust and Do pictures **(Reproducible 3B)**. Make enough copies so there is one small picture for each child. You may need to have more than one of the same picture. Cut the pictures apart. Put all the pictures inside a paper bag. Have the children sit in a circle.

Say: We can trust God and do what God wants us to do. Let's think about some of the things God wants us to do.

Have the children start passing the bag around the circle.

Say: Stop! What does God want us to do?

Have the child holding the bag reach inside and pull out a picture. Show the picture to the children.

Say: God wants us to *(name whatever the picture represents).*

Continue until all the pictures are removed from the bag. Pictures include:

Heart: love God and love one another
Bible: hear stories from the Bible
Musical instruments: praise God
Shaking hands: be kind to one another, be friendly
Crayons: share with one another
Praying hands: pray

Supplies

Reproducible 3B, paper bag

Roll a Prayer

Have the children sit in a circle with their legs spread out in front of them.

Say: We can do one of the things God wants us to do right now. We can pray.

Roll the ball to a child.

Say: Thank you, God, for *(child's name).* **Amen.**

Have the child roll the ball back to you. Repeat with each child in the circle.

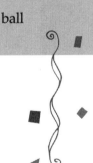

Supplies

ball

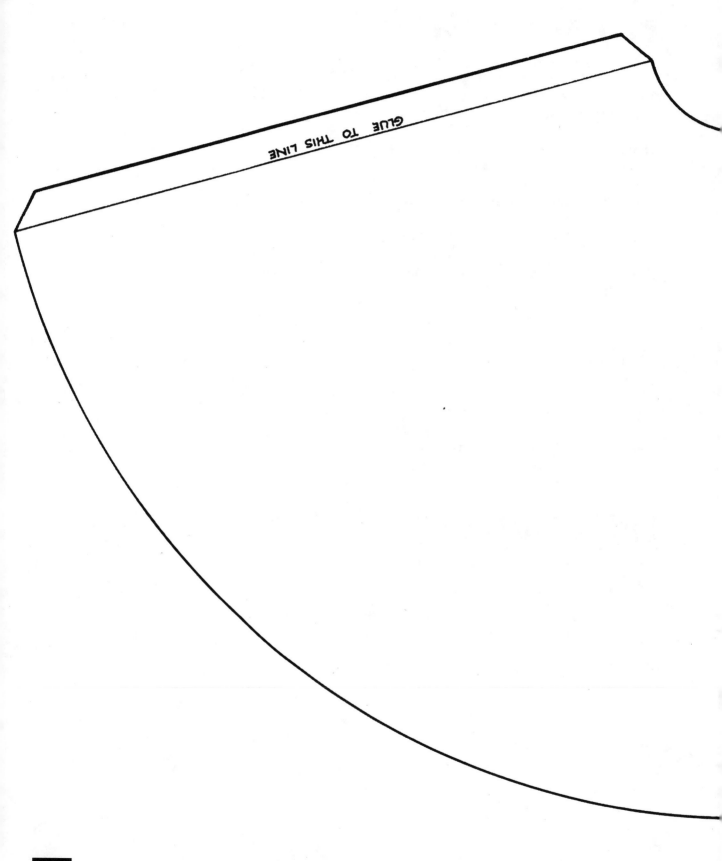

GLUE TO THIS LINE

REPRODUCIBLE 3B

All-in-One
BIBLE PRESCHOOL
FUN

Noah

Bible Verse

Trust in the LORD.
Psalm 37:3

Bible Story

Genesis 6:9–7:17, 24–8:22; 9:13

In the story of Noah, God destroyed the world with a flood. God told Noah to build an ark to save his family and the animals. Noah obeyed God, built the ark, and gathered two of every animal. When the flood was over, God promised Noah that God would never again send a flood to destroy humankind. The rainbow set in the clouds was a reminder of God's promise.

The world had become so evil, God decided to start over with creation. God selected Noah and his family to be part of this new beginning because Noah was faithful to God and trusted in God.

The ark was a kind of houseboat. It was built of gopher wood and had three decks. It was very large, 450 feet long. That is longer than a football field! It was 75 feet wide and 45 feet tall. The Scriptures only mention one door and one window.

The rainbow was a symbol of the covenant between God and the earth. It is a covenant that reaches from the time of Noah to future generations. In this covenant God promised to never again destroy all life with a flood. God promised that the world would be orderly and dependable.

As long as the earth endures,
    seedtime and harvest, cold and
        heat,
summer and winter, day and
        night,
    shall not cease. (Genesis 8:22)

The story of God destroying the world can be frightening for young children, particularly when so many floods are reported on national television. Because we want children to know that God is a loving and caring God, this lesson focuses on how Noah trusted God to take care of him, his family, and the animals, rather than the destruction of the world. With this focus the rainbow becomes a reminder of God's promise to care for us.

We can trust God to take care of us.

If time is limited, we recommend those activities that are noted in **boldface**. Depending on your time and the number of children, you may be able to include more activities.

ACTIVITY	TIME	SUPPLIES	
Ark Art	**10 minutes**	**Reproducible 4A, crayons**	JOIN THE FUN
Two by Two	10 minutes	Reproducible 4A, tape	
Rainbow Romp	5 minutes	different colors of ribbons or crepe paper streamers, scissors, tape	BIBLE STORY FUN
Bible Story: The Very Big Boat	**10 minutes**	**different colors of ribbons or crepe paper streamers, scissors, tape**	
Bible Verse Fun	**5 minutes**	**Bible**	
Rainbow Run	10 minutes	Reproducibles 4A and 4B, different colors of ribbons or crepe paper streamers, scissors, tape, crayons	
Two by Two Snack	10 minutes	Reproducible 4A, napkins, animal crackers	LIVE THE FUN
Roll a Prayer	**5 minutes**	**ball**	

Ark Art

Photocopy the ark **(Reproducible 4A)**. Let the children color the ark however they wish.

Say: Our Bible story is about a man named Noah. God told Noah to build a big boat. The boat is called an ark. God told Noah to bring two of every animal onto the ark. Noah trusted God and did what God told him to do.

Two by Two

Have the children move to an open area of the room. Tape the ark pictures **(Reproducible 4A)** on the floor in another area of the room.

Say the following rhyme:

> **Two by two,**
> **Two by two,**
> **Let's all be animals**
> **Two by two.**
> **Let's be** (*name an animal*).

Have the children pretend to move like that animal. Repeat the refrain several times, changing the last line to name a different animal.

Ask: What is your favorite animal?

Repeat the refrain once again, ending with: **Let's be our favorite animal.**

Encourage the children to move like their favorite animals. As the children are moving, touch the children on the shoulder two at a time. Tell the children to pretend that they are animals going into the ark. Have the children go to their ark pictures and sit down.

Say: God told Noah to bring his family and two of every animal on the boat. Noah and his family trusted God to take care of them on the boat.

> **We can trust God to take care of us.**

Rainbow Romp

Cut several different colors of ribbons or crepe paper streamers into 12-inch lengths. Gather all the ribbons or streamers together. Wrap tape around one of the ends to make a rainbow streamer.

Supplies

different colors of ribbons or crepe paper streamers, scissors, tape

Come, follow me on a rainbow romp.
We'll step, step, step and stomp, stomp, stomp.
(Wave the rainbow streamer.)

Let's step, step, step,
Step, step, step to our story.
(Step around the room.)

Come, follow me on a rainbow romp.
We'll step, step, step and stomp, stomp, stomp.
(Wave the rainbow streamer.)

Let's stomp, stomp, stomp,
Stomp, stomp, stomp to our story.
(Stomp around the room.)

Come, follow me on a rainbow romp.
We'll step, step, step and stomp, stomp, stomp.
(Wave the rainbow streamer.)

Let's tip, tip, toe,
Tip, tip, toe to our story.
(Walk on tiptoes.)

Come, follow me on a rainbow romp.
We'll step, step, step and stomp, stomp, stomp.
(Wave the rainbow streamer.)

(Speak in a quiet voice.)
Let's tip, tip, toe,
Tip, tip, toe to our story.
(Walk on tiptoes.)

(Continue to speak in a quiet voice.)
Come, follow me on a rainbow romp.
We'll step, step, step and stomp, stomp, stomp.
(Wave the rainbow streamer.)

(Whisper.)
Let's sit, sit, sit,
Sit, sit, sit for our story.
(Have the children sit down in your story area.)

Say: Today our Bible story is about a man named Noah. There is a big boat, lots of animals, and a rainbow in our story about Noah. Noah trusted God.

We can trust God to take care of us.

The Very Big Boat

by Daphna Flegal

Have the children do the motions and repeat the sounds after you each time they appear in the story. Have the rainbow streamer (see page 43) where you can easily reach it.

"Noah," said God, "I want you to build a very big boat." (*Spread arms as wide as you can.*) Noah obeyed God.

Zzz-zzz. Zzz-zzz. (*Pretend to use a saw.*) Noah cut the wood to build the very big boat.

"Baam baam. Baam baam," went the hammer. (*Curl one hand into a fist. Pound the fist into the palm of the other hand.*)

Finally the very big boat (*Spread arms as wide as you can.*) was finished.

Baa-baa. Noah brought two sheep into the very big boat. (*Spread arms wide.*)

Moo-moo. Noah brought two cows into the very big boat. (*Spread arms wide.*)

Roar-roar. Noah brought two lions into the very big boat. (*Spread arms wide.*)

Squeak-squeak. Noah brought two mice into the very big boat. (*Spread arms wide.*)

Quack-quack. Noah brought two ducks into the very big boat. (*Spread arms wide.*)

Neigh-neigh. Noah brought two horses into the very big boat. (*Spread arms wide.*)

Coo-coo. Noah brought two doves into the very big boat. (*Spread arms wide.*)

Baa. Roar. Quack. The very big boat (*Spread arms wide.*) was full of animals.

Spitter spatter. It started to rain. **Spitter spatter.** It rained and rained. **Spitter spatter.** It rained for forty days and forty nights.

Moo. Squeak. Neigh. Noah, his family, and all the animals were safe and dry inside the very big boat. (*Spread arms wide.*)

Shh-shh. The rain stopped.

Coo-coo. Noah sent a dove out of the very big boat. (*Spread arms wide.*) The dove did not return. Noah knew it was safe to leave the boat.

Baa. Roar. Squeak. All the animals left the very big boat. (*Spread arms wide.*)

Oooh-oooh. Noah and his family looked up into the sky. They saw streaks of red, orange, yellow, green, blue, and purple colors that stretched across the sky. It was a rainbow. (*Wave the rainbow streamers.*)

"I promise that I will always care for you," said God. "I have placed my rainbow across the clouds to help you remember my promise."

Oooh-ooh. Noah and his family looked at the rainbow. (*Wave the rainbow streamers.*) Noah knew he could trust God's promises.

Bible Verse Fun

Choose a child to hold the Bible open to Psalm 37:3.

Say: The story of Noah and the very big boat is from our Bible. Noah trusted God.

> ## We can trust God to take care of us.

Say the Bible verse, "Trust in the LORD" (Psalm 37:3), for the children. Have the children repeat the Bible verse after you

Help the children learn the Bible verse by singing. Sing the words printed below to the tune of "Do You Know the Muffin Man?"

> We can say the Bible verse,
> the Bible verse, the Bible verse.
> We can say the Bible verse,
> It's "Trust in the LORD."

Sing the song printed below to the tune of "Old MacDonald." Let the children suggest additional animals.

A Man Named Noah

A man name Noah built an ark,
'Cause he trusted God.
And on this ark he had two doves,
'Cause he trusted God.
With a coo, coo, here,
And a coo, coo, there
Here a coo, there a coo,
Everywhere a coo, coo.
A man name Noah built an ark,
'Cause he trusted God.

A man name Noah built an ark,
'Cause he trusted God.
And on this ark he had two horses,
'Cause he trusted God.
With a neigh, neigh, here,
And a neigh, neigh, there
Here a neigh, there a neigh,
Everywhere a neigh, neigh.
A man name Noah built an ark,
'Cause he trusted God.

A man name Noah built an ark,
'Cause he trusted God.
And on this ark he had two pigs,
'Cause he trusted God.
With an oink, oink, here,
And an oink, oink, there
Here an oink, there an oink,
Everywhere an oink, oink.
A man name Noah built an ark,
'Cause he trusted God.

A man name Noah built an ark,
'Cause he trusted God.
And on this ark he had two snakes,
'Cause he trusted God.
With a ssss, ssss, here,
And a ssss, ssss, there
Here a ssss, there a ssss,
Everywhere a ssss, ssss.
A man name Noah built an ark,
'Cause he trusted God.

Supplies

Reproducibles 4A and 4B, different colors of ribbons or crepe paper streamers, scissors, tape, crayons

Rainbow Run

Make one copy of the ark picture (**Reproducible 4A**) for this activity. Photocopy the rainbow picture (**Reproducible 4B**) for each child.

Choose three different colors of crayons. Hold the crayons together so that the tips of the crayons are even. Wrap the crayons with tape to make a set of rainbow crayons. Make a set for each child.

Say: God told Noah to build a very big boat. Then God told Noah to bring his family and two of every animal onto the boat. Noah trusted God to take care of his family and the animals on the boat. It rained and rained, but Noah, his family, and the animals were safe on the boat. When the rain stopped, Noah and his family saw something in the sky. It helped them remember that God promised to take care of them.

Ask: What did Noah and his family see in the sky after the rain stopped? (*a rainbow*)

Give each child a rainbow picture. Let the children color their pictures with the rainbow crayons.

Say: The rainbow can help us remember that we can trust God to take care of us.

Place the rainbow pictures in a rainbow arch on the floor on one side of the room. Set the rainbow streamer (see page 43) in front of the rainbow pictures. Tape the ark picture on the floor on the other side of the room. Have the children stand behind the ark. Make sure the space between the ark picture and the rainbow pictures is clear. Choose one child to be the rainbow runner.

Say: Rainbow runner, run to the rainbow.

Have the rainbow runner run across the room to the rainbow, pick up the streamer, and run back to the ark picture, waving the streamers.

Have the rainbow runner hold the streamer above the ark picture and say the Bible verse, "Trust in the LORD" (Psalm 37:3). Return the rainbow streamer to the rainbow.

Give each child a turn. Vary the game by changing how the children move to the rainbow:
Rainbow runner, hop to the rainbow.
Rainbow runner, march to the rainbow.
Rainbow runner, crawl to the rainbow.

46

Two by Two Snack

Supplies

Reproducible 4A, napkins, animal crackers

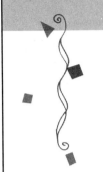

Photocopy the ark picture **(Reproducible 4A)** for each child to use as a place mat for a snack.

Choose a child to hand out napkins. Place two animal crackers on each child's ark picture. Help the children identify the animals.

Say: God told Noah to bring two of every kind of animal on the very big boat. Noah did what God told him to do. Noah knew that God would take care of his family and the animals on the boat.

We can trust God to take care of us.

Sing the song "A Man Named Noah" (see page 45) once again and use the animals represented by the crackers in the song.

Pray: Thank you, God, for stories from the Bible. Thank you for animal crackers to eat. Amen.

Roll a Prayer

Supplies

ball

Have the children sit in a circle with their legs spread out in front of them.

Say: Noah trusted God. We can trust God to take care of us.

Roll the ball to a child.

Say: Thank you, God, for *(child's name)*. **Amen.**

Have the child roll the ball back to you. Repeat with each child in the circle.

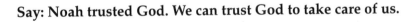

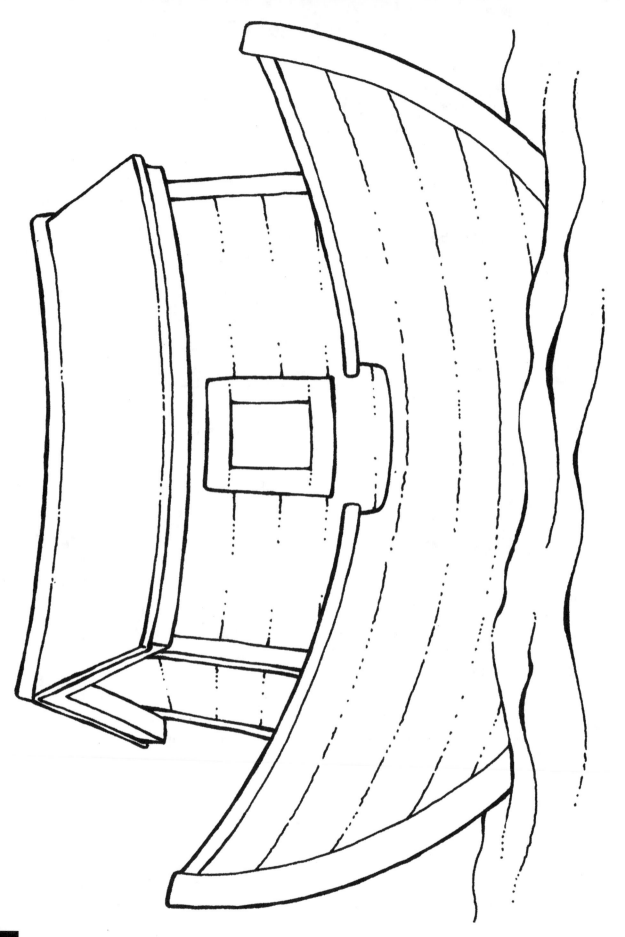

REPRODUCIBLE 4A

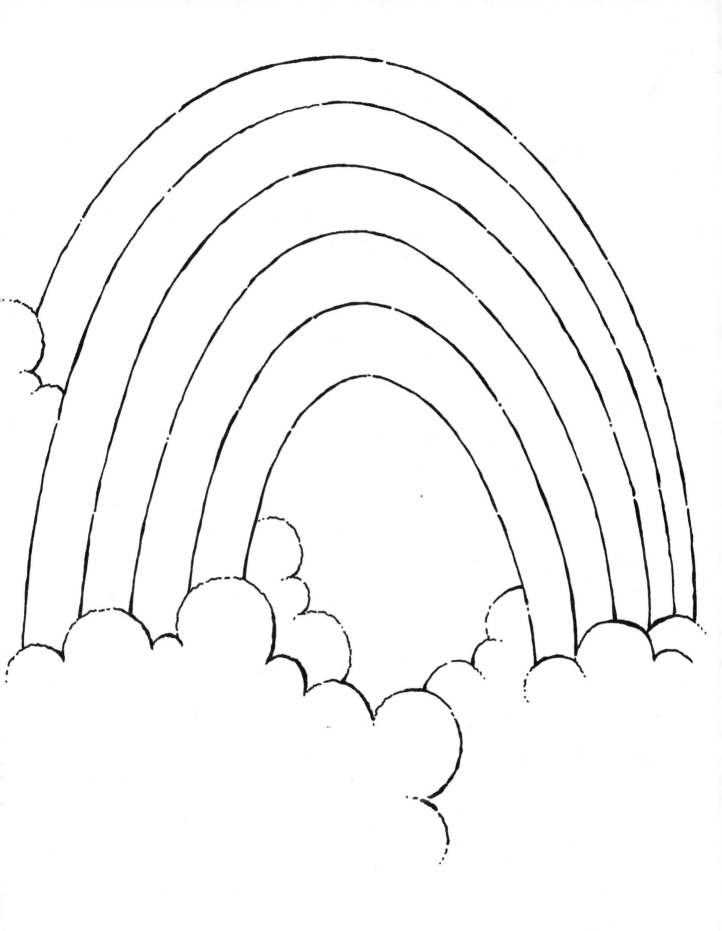

REPRODUCIBLE 4B

49

David

Bible Verse

I trust in God and am not afraid.

Psalm 56:4, GNT

Bible Story

1 Samuel 17:1-48

King David was the most beloved of all the kings of Israel. Not only was he a great leader, but he was also a statesman and a shrewd politician. Because of David, Israel grew from a loose tribal confederacy into a strong nation.

But how did it all happen? How did David, the ninth son of Jesse, a shepherd and a harp player, go from being a relative unknown to becoming King David, the royal champion of God?

David, even as a boy, was charming and charismatic. The stories about him that we find in the books of Samuel are similar to those that gather around any great national hero (like George Washington or Abraham Lincoln, for instance). The story the children will hear today is one of the more famous stories about David.

Goliath was a giant—a symbol of the threat of the Philistines. David on the other hand, was young—too young even to fight in the army. But David was not frightened at the prospect of facing Goliath. He relied on God to be with him in battle.

David's victory did more than simply defeat Goliath and the Philistines. David's victory gave glory to God. The victory showed the Israelites and the Philistines that God is so powerful that even a young boy with smooth stones and the power and strength of God in his heart can defeat a larger enemy.

Some parts of this story are too gruesome for young children. However, they will enjoy that a small boy was able to defeat a giant man. Our emphasis will be on David's trust that God would be with him.

Young children are often overlooked as being unimportant. But they are important to God. And with God's help, they, like the shepherd boy David, can do important things.

We can always trust God.

If time is limited, we recommend those activities that are noted in **boldface**. Depending on your time and the number of children, you may be able to include more activities.

ACTIVITY	TIME	SUPPLIES	
Big and Little Guys	10 minutes	Reproducible 5A, construction paper, glue, scissors	JOIN THE FUN
A Little Pouch	**10 minutes**	**Reproducible 5B, scissors, brown grocery bags, paper punch, yarn, tape**	
Rainbow Romp	5 minutes	different colors of ribbons or crepe paper streamers, scissors, tape	BIBLE STORY FUN
Bible Story: David and Goliath	**10 minutes**	**pouches from "A Little Pouch" activity (Reproducible 5B)**	
Bible Verse Fun	**10 minutes**	**Bible**	
Finger Play Fun	5 minutes	None	
Big and Little Game	5 minutes	None	
Always Trusting	5 minutes	None	LIVE THE FUN
Roll a Prayer	**5 minutes**	**ball**	

Supplies

Reproducible 5A, construction paper, glue, scissors

Big and Little Guys

Photocopy and cut apart the figures of David and Goliath **(Reproducible 5A)** for each child. Give each child the two figures. Let the child glue the figures onto a piece of construction paper.

Ask: Which person is the biggest? the smallest?

Say: Our Bible story is about David and Goliath. David was a shepherd boy. He watched over the family's sheep. He is the smallest person on your paper. But he was not too small to do what God wanted him to do.

Say: Goliath was a giant. He is the biggest person on your paper. He was very strong. He thought he was very important. Little David fought big Goliath, but David was not afraid because David trusted God.

We can always trust God.

Supplies

Reproducible 5B, scissors, brown grocery bags, paper punch, yarn, tape

A Little Pouch

Photocopy and cut apart the pattern for the shepherd's pouch **(Reproducible 5B)**. Cut a pouch from a brown paper grocery bag for each child. Using the sides of the grocery bags, cut out shoulder straps for the pouches.

Give each child a pouch. Show the children how to fold the pouches to form pockets. Help the children use a paper punch to punch holes around the edges.

Cut a 2-foot length of yarn for each child. Wrap tape around one end. Tape the other end of the yarn inside the pouch near the top right hole.

Show the children how to sew the sides of the pouch by going in and out of the holes with the yarn. When the pocket is sewn, tape down the loose end of the yarn. Trim if necessary. Help the children staple a shoulder strap onto the pouch. Encourage the children to wear their pouches.

Say: David was a shepherd. He watched over his family's sheep. Sometimes he had to chase big animals like lions or bears away from the sheep. But he didn't have big weapons. He used a slingshot. He would put stones in the slingshot and then throw the stones at the lion or bear. David carried his slingshot and stones in a leather pouch.

Rainbow Romp

Supplies

different colors of ribbons or crepe paper streamers, scissors, tape

Cut several different colors of ribbons or crepe paper streamers into 12-inch lengths. Gather all the ribbons or streamers together. Wrap tape around one of the ends to make a rainbow streamer.

Come, follow me on a rainbow romp.
We'll step, step, step and stomp, stomp, stomp.
(Wave the rainbow streamer.)

Let's step, step, step,
Step, step, step to our story.
(Step around the room.)

Come, follow me on a rainbow romp.
We'll step, step, step and stomp, stomp, stomp.
(Wave the rainbow streamer.)

Let's stomp, stomp, stomp,
Stomp, stomp, stomp to our story.
(Stomp around the room.)

Come, follow me on a rainbow romp.
We'll step, step, step and stomp, stomp, stomp.
(Wave the rainbow streamer.)

Let's stomp, stomp, stomp,
Stomp, stomp, stomp to our story.
(Stomp your feet as you walk.)

Come, follow me on a rainbow romp.
We'll step, step, step and stomp, stomp, stomp.
(Wave the rainbow streamer.)

(Speak in a quiet voice.)
Let's tip, tip, toe,
Tip, tip, toe to our story.
(Walk on tiptoes.)

(Continue to speak in a quiet voice.)
Come, follow me on a rainbow romp.
We'll step, step, step and stomp, stomp, stomp.
(Wave the rainbow streamer.)

(Whisper.)
Let's sit, sit, sit,
Sit, sit, sit for our story.
(Have children sit down in your story area.)

Say: Today our Bible story is about David and Goliath. David fought Goliath, David was not afraid because David trusted God. We can trust God to be with us when we are not afraid and when we are afraid.

We can always trust God.

David and Goliath

by Beth Parr

Have the children wear their shepherds' pouches (**Reproducible 5B**) *and join in with motions for the action words.*

Stomp, stomp, stomp.
(Stomp feet.)
Goliath was stomping his feet as he walked back and forth. Goliath was very tall, over nine feet tall. He was walking in front of King Saul's army.

Shout, shout, shout.
(Cup hands around mouth.)
Goliath shouted to the people in King Saul's army. "I am the best soldier. I am the strongest soldier. I can beat anyone in your army. Who will come and fight me?"

Shake, shake shake.
(Pretend to shake as though afraid.)
The men in King Saul's army were afraid of Goliath because he was so big and strong. They did not want to have to fight Goliath.

Hurry, hurry, hurry.
(Run in place.)
David hurried to take food to his brothers who were in King Saul's army. David was a young boy who took care of his father's sheep. He was not big and strong like Goliath.

Listen, listen, listen.
(Cup hands around ears.)
When David arrived at King Saul's camp, he heard Goliath yelling at the army. "Why is no one willing to fight Goliath?" David asked the soldiers. David's older brother was angry that David was asking questions and talking to the other soldiers. "You are too young to be there," he said to David. "Go home and take care of the sheep."

Come, come, come.
(Motion with hand.)
Some of the soldiers told King Saul about David. King Saul asked David to come see him. But when King Saul saw how young David was, he did not think David could fight Goliath.

Yes, yes, yes.
(Nod head.)
David knew that he could fight Goliath, and he could win. David trusted God, and was not afraid. King Saul finally said that David could try. He gave David his armor, his helmet, and his sword. These things were so big that David couldn't even walk.

Pick, pick, pick.
(Pretend to pick up stones and put them in your shepherd's pouch.)
David took off the armor and went to the stream. He picked up five smooth stones: 1, 2, 3, 4, 5. David put the stones in his leather bag and went to fight Goliath.

Ha, ha, ha!
(Pretend to laugh.)
When Goliath saw David, he laughed because David was so little. But David put one of the stones in his sling and threw it at the giant. The stone hit Goliath in the head, and Goliath fell down. Little David had beaten the giant Goliath. God was with David. David trusted God and was not afraid.

Adapted from "David and Goliath," *BibleZone Live@ Preschool: In the City of David*, © 2004 Abingdon Press.

Bible Verse Fun

Choose a child to hold the Bible open to Psalm 56:4.

Say: Our Bible story is about David and Goliath. David was not afraid of Goliath because David trusted God. We can trust God to be with us when we are not afraid and when we are afraid. We can always trust God.

> ## We can always trust God.

Say the Bible verse, "I trust in God and am not afraid" (Psalm 56:4, GNT), for the children. Have the children say the Bible verse after you.

Help the children learn the Bible verse by singing. Sing the words printed below to the tune of "God Is So Good."

> "I trust in God.
> I trust in God.
> I trust in God and am not afraid."

Sing the song printed below to the tune of "The Farmer in the Dell."

David Trusted God

O, David trusted God.
O, David trusted God.
When he watched his father's sheep,
(Put hand over forehead to shade eyes.)
O David trusted God.

O, David trusted God.
O, David trusted God.
When he took his brothers' food,
(Walk in place.)
O David trusted God.

O, David trusted God.
O, David trusted God.
When he saw Goliath stomp,
(Stomp feet.)
O David trusted God.

O, David trusted God.
O, David trusted God.
When he looked for five small stones,
(Pretend to pick up stones)
O David trusted God.

O, David trusted God.
O, David trusted God.
When the sling went 'round and 'round,
(Pretend to twirl sling.)
O David trusted God.

O, David trusted God.
O, David trusted God.
When he saw Goliath fall,
(Clap hands on the word "fall.")
O David trusted God.

Finger Play Fun

Say: In our Bible Story today, we heard about David and Goliath. Let's tell the story again. Just say what I say and do what I do.

Here is Goliath: "Yo, ho, ho!"
(Hold up thumb on left hand.)
Here is David: "No, no, no!"
(Hold up little finger on your right hand.)
David uses his sling to throw a rock.
(Move your little finger in a circle.)
And it hits Goliath with a...thwock.
(Put thumb down.)
© 2007 Cokesbury

Big and Little Game

Have the children move to one side of the room.

Say: Our Bible story is about David and Goliath. David was little and Goliath was very big. But when David fought Goliath, David was not afraid because David trusted God. We can trust God to be with us when we are not afraid and when we are afraid. We can always trust God.

We can always trust God.

Have the children stay where they are as you move to the other side of the room. Make sure the area is clear between you and the children.

Say: I'm going to ask you to take big Goliath steps or little David steps across the room toward me. If I give you David steps, then before you step you have to say our Bible verse, "I trust in God and am not afraid" (Psalm 56:4, GNT).

Have the children move as a group. Tell them what kind and how many steps to take. For example: Take three Goliath steps; or take two David steps. You will probably have to remind the children to say the Bible verse before taking the David steps.

Always Trusting

Supplies

None

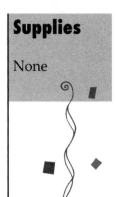

Have the children sit down in a circle.

Say: Let's play a game. I'm going to name times when we might be afraid. If we can trust God when we are afraid, I'll tell you a motion to do.

If we can trust God when we are lonely, stand up, turn around, and sit down.

If we can trust God when we are frightened by a storm, clap your hands two times.

If we can trust God when we are afraid of the dark, jump up and down.

If we can trust God when we miss our mom or dad, shout, "Hooray!"

If we can trust God when we are trying something new, pat your knees.

If we can always trust God to be with us, and take care of us, stand up and wave your hands in the air.

Say: David knew that God was with him. He was not afraid to face Goliath. We know that God is always with us. God is with us when we are afraid, and God is with us when we are not afraid.

© 2004 Abingdon Press

We can always trust God.

Roll a Prayer

Supplies

ball

Have the children sit in a circle with their legs spread out in front of them.

Say: David trusted God. We can always trust God.

Roll the ball to a child.

Say: Thank you, God, for *(child's name)*. Amen.

Have the child roll the ball back to you. Repeat with each child in the circle.

REPRODUCIBLE 5A

All-in-One
BIBLE PRESCHOOL
FUN

Miriam and Moses

Bible Verse

Love one another.

John 15:17

Bible Story

Exodus 2:4-10

Moses' mother put her baby in a basket and set him afloat on the Nile River in order to protect him and keep him safe.

Miriam was the older sister of Moses and Aaron. She watched over Moses as he floated in his basket, and she brought Moses' own mother to the pharaoh's daughter to help raise Moses. Miriam grew to be one of the Israelite leaders. She sang a song (Exodus 15:20-21) that expressed the celebration of the Israelites crossing the Red Sea as they made their exodus from Egypt.

Baby Moses was in need of protection from Pharaoh. The Israelites had lived in Egypt for almost 370 years. The story of how Joseph saved Egypt from the famine had been forgotten by the Egyptians. The new pharaoh had forced the Israelites to become slaves. In spite of their slavery the number of Israelites living in Egypt kept growing. The new pharaoh began to fear the Israelites because of their great numbers. He ordered that all Hebrew male babies were to be drowned in the Nile River.

Moses' mother wanted to hide baby Moses because of Pharaoh's order. She made the basket from bulrushes that grew along the edge of the Nile River. After she had woven the basket, she made it watertight by covering it with bitumen. Bitumen is similar to asphalt. Moses' mother then placed him in the basket and put the basket in the river. Sister Miriam watched, hidden in the reeds.

The princess who found Moses was probably the daughter of one of the pharaoh's concubines. She would have raised Moses with others in the harem. Moses would have received a good education as a member of the princess' family.

The focus of today's telling of this familiar Bible story is love. Moses' mother showed love when she tried to protect her son. Sister Miriam showed love when she watched over her brother. The princess showed love when she took Moses out of the river and raised him as part of her family. Help your children think of ways they can show love to their families today.

We can show love to our families.

If time is limited, we recommend those activities that are noted in **boldface**. Depending on your time and the number of children, you may be able to include more activities.

ACTIVITY	TIME	SUPPLIES	
Lilypad Leap	**10 minutes**	**Reproducibles 6A and 6B, crayons, scissors, clear tape baby doll, masking tape, doll blanket or scarf**	JOIN THE FUN
Rock the Baby	10 minutes	baby doll	
Watch It!	10 minutes	2 towels or 2 pieces of fabric; 5 or 6 different items such as a box of crayons, book, toy, block, ball, or puzzle	BIBLE STORY FUN
Bible Story: Sister Miriam Watched	**10 minutes**	**basket (Reproducible 6B), baby doll**	
Bible Verse Fun	**5 minutes**	**Bible**	
Who Has the Baby?	10 minutes	basket (Reproducible 6B), baby doll	
Family Finger Fun	10 minutes	masking tape, ballpoint pen	LIVE THE FUN
Beanbag Prayers	**5 minutes**	**beanbag or crumpled paper ball**	

Supplies

Reproducibles 6A and 6B, crayons, scissors, clear tape baby doll, masking tape, doll blanket or scarf

Lilypad Leap

Photocopy the water lilies **(Reproducible 6A)** for each child. Copy extra pages so that you will have enough lilies to make a winding path around your room, ending in your story area.

Make one copy of the basket **(Reproducible 6B)**. Let the children who arrive early color the basket with crayons. Cut the corners of the basket along the dotted lines. Fold up and overlap each corner. Tape each corner together.

Give each child a water lily page. Let the children color the water lilies with crayons.

Say: Sometimes water lilies grow in rivers. There is a river in our Bible story today. Let's pretend to put our water lilies in a river. Collect the water lilies from the children. Make a path by placing the water lilies on the floor. Secure the water lilies with masking tape. Have the path wind through your room and end at your story area.

Wrap the baby doll with the doll blanket or scarf. Place the baby doll in the basket **(Reproducible 6B)** and set the basket at the end of the water lily path. This is to represent baby Moses floating on the Nile River.

Have the children move to the beginning of the water lily path.

Say: Let's pretend that we are frogs. Hop along the water lily path to find something special.

Encourage the children to hop like frogs as they follow the path to your story area.

Ask: What have you found? *(a baby in a basket)*

Say: The baby in the basket is baby Moses. Our Bible story today is about baby Moses. Moses' mother put him in a basket to keep him safe. Baby Moses had a sister named Miriam. We will learn how Miriam showed love to her baby brother.

We can show love to our families.

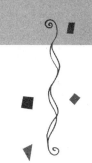

Supplies

baby doll

Rock the Baby

Have the children sit down in your story area. Show the children the baby doll.

Say: Today our story is about baby Moses and his sister Miriam. Miriam loved baby Moses and helped to keep him safe. What are some ways we take care of babies? *(feed them, hold them, change their clothes, love them, make sure they are safe)* Babies like to be held and rocked. Let's take turns rocking baby Moses.

Let the children take turns rocking the baby doll. Softly sing or say the following lullaby as the children hold the doll. The tune is "Hot Cross Buns."

Go to sleep,
Go to sleep,
While I rock you, baby Moses,
Go to sleep.

Watch It!

Supplies

2 towels or 2 pieces of fabric; 5 or 6 different items such as a box of crayons, book, toy, block, ball, or puzzle

Spread out a towel or piece of fabric on the floor. Place five or six different items on the towel or fabric.

Say: Let's all be watchers. Look at the things I have placed on the cloth.

Cover the items with a second towel or piece of cloth. Have the children cover their eyes with their hands. Slip one of the items out from under the fabric and place it behind your back. Have the children uncover their eyes. Choose a child to take the covering cloth off the items.

Say: Look at the things on the cloth. What is missing?

Have the children remember what item is missing from the items. When the children have named the item, show the children the item hidden behind your back. Repeat the game and remove a different item each time.

Say: Today our Bible story is about baby Moses and his sister Miriam. Miriam watched baby Moses to help keep him safe. When Miriam watched her baby brother, she was showing love.

We can show love to our families.

Sister Miriam Watched

by Daphna Flegal

Use the baby doll and basket **(Reproducible 6B)** *as you tell this story. Follow the suggestions printed in italics and encourage the children to do the motions with you.*

Rock, rock, rock. *(Rock the baby doll in your arms. Have the children pretend to rock a baby.)* Mother rocked baby Moses gently in her arms. Then Mother put baby Moses into a basket. *(Put the baby doll in the basket. Set the basket on the floor.)*

Sister Miriam watched. *(Point to your eyes.)* She loved baby Moses.

Splash, splash, splash. *(Make rippling motions with fingers.)* Mother carefully placed the basket at the edge of the river.

Sister Miriam watched. *(Point to your eyes.)* She knew Mother was hiding baby Moses in the basket to keep him safe from Pharaoh.

Splash, splash, splash. *(Make rippling motions with fingers.)* The basket floated on the water.

Sister Miriam watched. *(Point to your eyes.)* She wanted to help keep baby Moses safe. Miriam hid behind the tall grasses at the edge of the river where she could see baby Moses.

Splash, splash, splash. *(Make rippling motions with fingers.)* Soon Pharaoh's daughter waded into the river to take a bath.

Sister Miriam watched. *(Point to your eyes.)* She knew Pharaoh's daughter was a princess.

Splash, splash, splash. *(Make rippling motions with fingers.)* The princess saw the basket floating on the river.

Sister Miriam watched. *(Point to your eyes.)* She saw the princess open the basket and find baby Moses.

Splash, splash, splash. *(Make rippling motions with fingers.)* Miriam waded in the water to the princess. She knew that the princess would keep baby Moses safe from Pharaoh.

"Do you want me to find a woman to feed and help care for the baby?" Miriam asked the princess?

"Yes," said the princess. "Go and find someone."

Splash, splash, splash. *(Make rippling motions with fingers.)* Miriam waded out of the water. She ran to get Moses' own mother and brought her to the princess.

Rock, rock, rock. *(Rock the baby doll in your arms. Have the children pretend to rock a baby.)* Mother gently rocked baby Moses in her arms once again.

Sister Miriam watched. *(Point to your eyes.)* She was happy baby Moses would be safe with the princess and Moses' mother. The princess, Moses' mother, and Miriam loved and cared for Moses as he grew.

© 1997 Abingdon Press.

Bible Verse Fun

Choose a child to hold the Bible open to John 15:17.

Say: Miriam loved her baby brother Moses. She watched over him and helped keep him safe.

> ## We can show love to our families.

Say the Bible verse, "Love one another" (John 15:17), for the children. Have the children repeat the Bible verse after you.

Help the children learn the Bible verse by singing. Sing the words printed below to the tune of "The Wheels on the Bus."

O "Love one another,"
Love, love, love.
Love, love, love.
Love, love, love.
O "Love one another,"
Love, love, love.
"Love one another."

Sing the song printed below to the tune of "Are You Sleeping?"

Where's Baby Moses?

Where's Baby Moses?
Where's Baby Moses?
Here I am. Here I am.
Floating on the river, floating on the river.
Please find me. Please find me.

Where's Moses' mother?
Where's Moses' mother?
Here I am. Here I am.
Taking care of Moses, taking care of Moses
I love him. I love him.

Where's the princess?
Where's the princess?
Here I am. Here I am.
Walking to the river. Walking to the river.
For a bath. For a bath.

Where is Miriam?
Where is Miriam?
Here I am. Here I am.
Watching over Moses, watching over Moses
Shh, don't cry. Shh, don't cry.

Words: Sue Downing
© 1989 Graded Press

Supplies

basket (Reproducible 6B), baby doll

Who Has the Baby?

Have the children stand in a circle. Place the baby doll in the basket **(Reproducible 6B)** and place the basket in the middle of the circle.

Choose one child to be *Miriam*. Have *Miriam* go to the middle of the circle and close his or her eyes.

While *Miriam* cannot see, choose another child to be the *princess*. Have the *princess* quietly take the baby out of the basket and hold it.

Say:

> Miriam, Miriam,
> Who has the baby?
> Guess who it is today.
>
> Miriam, Miriam,
> Who has the baby?
> Listen to that person say,
> "Love one another."

Have the *princess* repeat the Bible verse: **Love one another (John 15:17)**.

Miriam tries to guess who is holding the baby. Have *Miriam* open his or her eyes and have the *princess* put the baby back in the basket. Continue the game, giving each child an opportunity to be Miriam and the princess.

Say: In today's Bible story Miriam watched over her baby brother Moses to help keep him safe. When Miriam watched over baby Moses, she was showing love.

We can show love to our families.

Talk with the children about ways they can show love to their families. Be ready with suggestions such as helping mother or father, saying "I love you," playing with a baby brother or sister, setting the table, taking out the trash, putting away toys, getting along with older brothers or sisters, visiting with grandparents, and so forth.

Family Finger Fun

Supplies

masking tape, ballpoint pen

Help each child determine the number of people who are in her or his family. Tear off small pieces of masking tape. Cover the ends of the child's fingers with a masking tape strip, one for each member of the child's family. Use a ballpoint pen to draw a simple face on the tape pieces.

Repeat the following rhyme for the children. Have the children hold up their fingers and count the people in their families in response to the rhyme. (This activity can also be done without the masking tape. Just have the children hold up a finger for each person in their families.)

Who's in my family?
Just look and see.
There's (*Have the child hold up his or her fingers.*
Help the child name each person in her or his family.)
And me!

I love my family.
Just look and see.
I love (*Have the child hold up his or her fingers.*
Help the child name each person in her or his family.)
And they love me!

Beanbag Prayers

Supplies

beanbag or crumpled paper ball

Have the children sit in a circle. Provide a beanbag or crumple paper into a ball.

Say: Moses' mother Miriam and the princess all showed love to baby Moses.

> ## We can show love to our families.

Say: One way we can show love to our families is by praying for our families. Let's pray to God right now.

Call a child by name. Have the child hold his or her arms like a basket. Toss the beanbag in the child's "basket."

Say: Thank you, God, for (*child's name*) **and** (*child's name*)**'s family. Amen.**

REPRODUCIBLE 6A

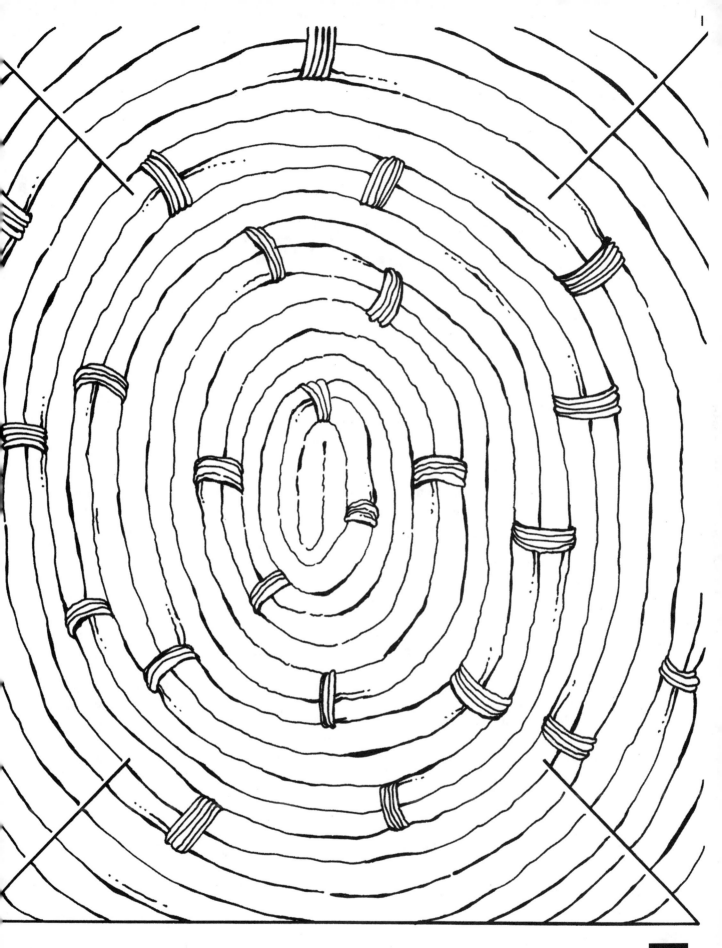

Esther

Bible Verse

Love one another.

John 15:17

Bible Story

Esther 1:1–7:10

The story of Esther is a story of courage. Esther was chosen to be the new queen of King Ahasuerus, the king of Persia, because of her great beauty. But Esther was more than beautiful; she was courageous.

Haman, the king's prime minister, considered himself to be a very important person, so important that he decided that everyone should worship him. When Mordecai, Esther's cousin, refused, Haman claimed that all the Jews, including Mordecai, were disloyal to the king. He devised a plot to convince the king to order the death of all Jews. When Haman plotted to destroy the Jews, Esther helped her people at the risk of her own life.

Esther went to the king's chambers without being invited, a deed that was punishable by death. But the king felt kindness toward Esther, and Esther invited the king and Haman to a banquet. At that banquet Esther told the king she was a Jew. Then Esther exposed Haman's plot and asked the king to help the Jews.

When the king learned about Haman's plot to kill the Jews, he became enraged. The king ordered Haman killed the same way Haman had planned to kill Mordecai.

Young children will not understand all the political intrigue that is part of Esther's story. They can, however, understand that Esther was a woman who did something brave to help her people.

Young children want to help. Offer your children opportunities to help in your classroom. Have the children help pick up toys, hand out napkins or reproducible sheets, and hand out crayons or other supplies. Make it a habit to compliment the children each time they help.

Also offer opportunities for your children to help others outside of your classroom. Collect food, clothing, or money for church mission projects. Lead your children in praying for friends and family members who are sick. Remind your children that when we help others, we are helping God.

We show love when we help others.

If time is limited, we recommend those activities that are noted in **boldface**. Depending on your time and the number of children, you may be able to include more activities.

ACTIVITY	TIME	SUPPLIES	
Jazzy Jewels	10 minutes	colored drinking straws, safety scissors, yarn, tape	JOIN THE FUN
Crown Queen Esther	**10 minutes**	**Reproducibles 7A and 7B, scissors, tape**	
Royal Romp	5 minutes	construction paper or bulletin board border, scissors, tape	BIBLE STORY FUN
Bible Story: Queen Esther	**10 minutes**	**None**	
Bible Verse Fun	**10 minutes**	**Bible**	
Caring Crowns	5 minutes	Reproducible 7B, scissors, tape	
Queen Esther, Queen Esther	10 minutes	construction paper or bulletin board border, scissors, tape	
Ring Around the Queen	10 minutes	construction paper or bulletin board border, scissors, tape	LIVE THE FUN
Beanbag Prayers	**5 minutes**	**beanbag or crumpled paper ball**	

Supplies

colored drink-
ing straws,
safety scissors,
yarn, tape

Jazzy Jewels

Cut colored drinking straws into 1-inch pieces. Or let the children use safety scissors to cut the drinking straws into small pieces. Cutting drinking straws can be a successful cutting experience for young children.

Cut yarn into 36-inch lengths. Wrap one end of each length of yarn with tape to make the yarn easier to thread through the drinking straw pieces.

Say: Our Bible story today is about a woman named Esther. Esther became queen. Let's make jewelry for kings and queens.

Let the children make necklaces by stringing the drinking straw pieces onto the yarn. Encourage the children to wear their necklaces.

Say: Queen Esther was very brave. She helped her people. When Esther helped her people she was showing love.

We show love when we help others.

Supplies

Reproducibles
7A and 7B,
scissors, tape

Crown Queen Esther

Photocopy Esther's face **(Reproducible 7A)** and the crowns **(Reproducible 7B)**. Copy the crown page so that you have enough crowns for each child. Cut apart the crowns.

Display Esther's face on a wall, bulletin board, or door. Be sure to place the picture where the children can easily reach it. Give each child a crown.

Say: Our Bible story today is about a woman named Esther. Esther became queen. Let's put the crown on Queen Esther.

Play the game like "Pin the Tail on the Donkey." Have the children come one at a time to stand in front of Esther's face. Put a loop of masking tape on the back of the crowns. Have each child close his or her eyes. Let each child try to place the crown on top of Esther's head with his or her eyes closed.

After everyone has had a turn at the game, **say: Queen Esther was very brave. She helped her people. When Esther helped her people she was showing love.**

Royal Romp

Supplies

construction paper or bulletin board border, scissors, tape

Make a crown out of paper. Cut a piece of construction paper in half lengthwise. Tape the ends of the two halves together to make one long strip. Or use a strip of bulletin board border. Measure the strip around a child's head. Tape the ends together.

Say: Let's have a royal parade. Let's all follow Queen Esther.

Choose a child to be Queen Esther. Place the paper crown on the child's head. Hold the child's hand and lead the children around the room in a "Follow the Leader" game.

Wind the children around the room, circling chairs and tables to make the game more fun. Change how you move (walk, hop, tiptoe, march) and have the children copy your movements. As you move around the room, sing "Follow Me" to the tune of "London Bridge."

Follow Me
Follow me, for I am queen,
I am queen, I am queen.
Follow me, for I am queen.
I help my people.
(Stand still and wave like a beauty queen.)

If you have a small number of children, sing the song several times. After each time you stop and wave, choose a different child to be Queen Esther. Place the paper crown on that child's head.

If you have a large number of children and do not have time for every one to have a turn, play the game and be Queen Esther yourself.

When you finish the game, have everyone sit down in the story area.

Say: Today our Bible story is about a woman named Esther. Esther became a queen. She helped her people. When Esther helped her people she was showing love.

We show love when we help others.

Queen Esther

by Daphna Flegal

According to Jewish tradition, the story of Esther is told as a melodrama. Tell the children that you want them to help you tell today's Bible story.

Say: Our Bible story is about a very brave woman named Esther. Esther showed love by helping her people. Each time I say the name *Esther*, I want you to say, "Yea!" *(Practice with the children.)* **The story also has a bad man named Haman. Each time I say the name *Haman*, I want you to say, "Boo!"** *(Practice with the children. Then remind the children that it can be fun to boo the bad guy in the story, but it is unkind to boo people.)*

Esther was very beautiful. She was also kind and loving. She lived with her cousin. **Esther** and her cousin were Jews. They loved God.

One day the king decided to marry a new queen. **Esther** went with her cousin to the palace to meet the king. When the king met **Esther**, he chose her to be his new queen. She was very happy. **Esther** liked being the queen and living in the palace.

Haman worked for the king. He was a selfish man. **Haman** thought he was more important than other people. **Haman** did not like the Jews. He wanted to do something to hurt the Jews. **Haman** tricked the king into making a law to kill all people who were Jews.

Queen **Esther** and her cousin were very upset. They were Jewish. "You must help our people," her cousin told Queen **Esther**. "You must talk to the king."

"I'm afraid," said Queen **Esther**. "The king might decide to kill me."

"You must be brave," said her cousin.

Queen **Esther** decided she would be brave. She asked her people to pray for her. **Esther** knew that God wanted her to show love by helping her people.

She went to the king. **Esther** told him that she was a Jew. Queen **Esther** told the king about **Haman's** plan to kill all the Jews.

The king was very angry. He loved Queen **Esther**. He did not want the Jews killed. The king ordered his men to take **Haman** away. Queen **Esther** showed love when she helped her people.

Bible Verse Fun

Choose a child to hold the Bible open to John 15:17.

Say: The story of Esther is from our Bible. When Esther helped her people, she was showing love. When we help others, we show love.

 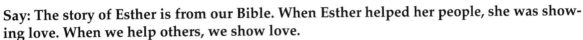

Say the Bible verse, "Love one another" (John 15:17), for the children. Have the children repeat the Bible verse after you.

Help the children learn the Bible verse by singing. Sing the words printed below to the tune of "The Wheels on the Bus."

O "Love one another,"
Love, love, love.
Love, love, love.
Love, love, love.
O "Love one another,"
Love, love, love.
"Love one another."

Sing the song printed below to the tune of "Did You Ever See a Lassie?"

Let Us Sing About Queen Esther

Let us sing about Queen Esther,
Queen Esther, Queen Esther,
Let us sing about Queen Esther,
for she was so brave.

She saved all her people
by telling on Haman.
Let us sing about Queen Esther,
for she was so brave.

Words: Sharilyn S. Adair
© 1997 Abingdon Press

Caring Crowns

Photocopy and cut out the crowns **(Reproducible 7B)**. You will need one crown for each child. Write each child's name on a crown.

Say: Queen Esther showed love when she helped her people. We can show love like Queen Esther.

> ## We show love when we help others.

Call each child up by name. Use masking tape to attach the crown onto the child's clothing.

Say: Queen *(or King as appropriate to gender, and then say the child's name)*, **you can help others.**

Queen Esther, Queen Esther

Make a crown out of paper. Cut a piece of construction paper in half lengthwise. Tape the ends of the two halves together to make one long strip. Or use a strip of bulletin board border. Measure the strip around a child's head. Tape the ends together.

Have the children move to open area of the room and sit down.

Choose one child to begin the game. This child will be Queen Esther. Have Queen Esther stand in front of the group. Place the paper crown on Queen Esther's head and then say the following rhyme.

> **Queen Esther, Queen Esther,**
> **You are so brave.**
> **What did you do**
> **Your people to save?**

Have the child choose a movement he or she wants to do such as jumping, hopping, clapping, marching, turning around, and so forth. You may need to make suggestions to the child.

Say: Queen Esther, *(name motion)*.

Have the child pretending to be Queen Esther begin the movement. Encourage the other children to follow. Choose another child to be Queen Esther. Repeat the game as the children show interest.

Ring Around the Queen

Make a crown out of paper. Cut a piece of construction paper in half lengthwise. Tape the ends of the two halves together to make one long strip. Or use a strip of bulletin board border. Measure the strip around a child's head. Tape the ends together.

Choose an open area of the room. Have the children sit on the floor in a circle. Choose one child to be Queen Ester. Place the crown on the child's head.

Have Queen Esther walk around the outside of the circle. Instruct Queen Esther to tap the head of a child seated in the circle and say one word of the Bible verse, "Love one another." Help the children remember the words.

Have Queen Esther continue around the circle, tapping a child with each word of the Bible verse. On the last word of the Bible verse, have the child who was tapped get up and chase Queen Esther around the circle until Queen Esther sits down in the space vacated by the child.

When the child is seated, **say: (***Child's name***) can help others. Thank you, God, for (***child's name***).**

Let the tapped child become the next Queen Esther. Place the paper crown on the new queen's head. Have the new Queen Esther continue the game, tapping a child with each word of the Bible verse. Play the game until every child has an opportunity to play Queen Esther.

Supplies

construction paper or bulletin board border, scissors, tape

Beanbag Prayers

Have the children sit in a circle. Provide a beanbag or crumple paper into a ball.

Say: Esther showed love by helping her people.

We show love when we help others.

Say: One way we show love and help others is by praying. We can pray for one other. Let's pray to God right now.

Call a child by name. Have the child hold his or her arms like a basket. Toss the beanbag in the child's "basket."

Say: Thank you, God, for (*child's name***). Amen.**

Supplies

beanbag or crumpled paper ball

REPRODUCIBLE 7A

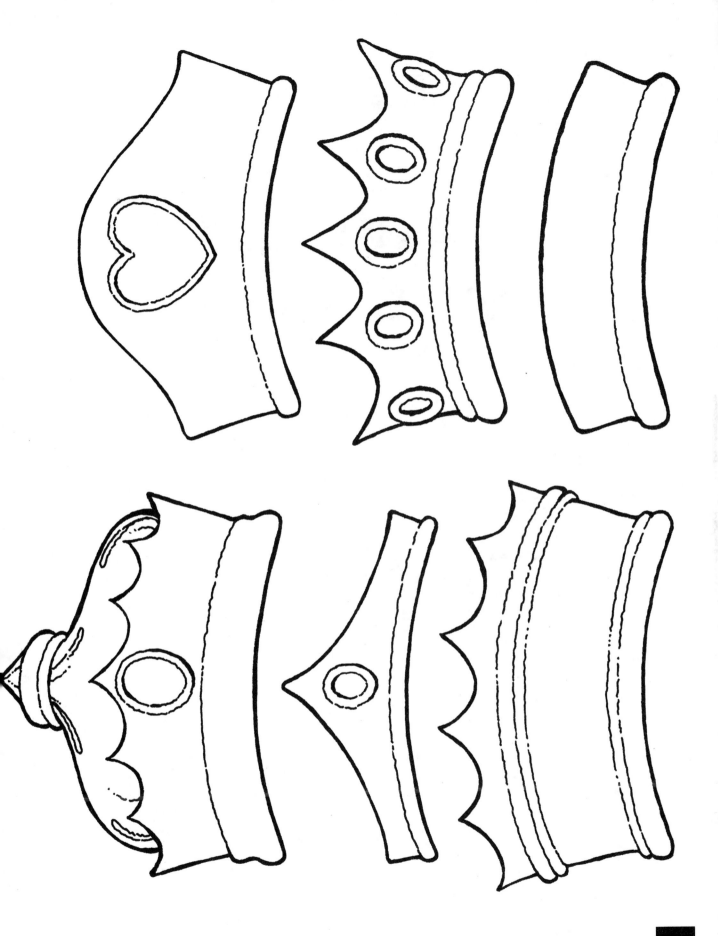

REPRODUCIBLE 7B

All-in-One

BIBLE PRESCHOOL

FUN

Jesus and the Children

Bible Verse

Let the children come to me.

Luke 18:16, GNT

Bible Story

Mark 10:13-16

This favorite Bible passage tells the story of Jesus' love and acceptance of children. Parents were bringing their children to be blessed by Jesus. The disciples tried to stop the children from bothering Jesus, but Jesus told the disciples to "let the little children come to me" (Mark 10:14).

Jesus was indignant when he stopped his friends from sending the children away. His attitude must have been hard for his friends to understand. Children, like women, had few personal rights in Bible times. Jesus' friends probably thought the children were not important enough to interrupt Jesus. After all, crowds of adults had come to hear Jesus teach. But Jesus had a way of turning around common practices. He must have surprised everyone when he stopped what he was doing to spend time with the children.

Jesus told the crowd gathered to hear him teach that the kingdom of God belongs to children. He wanted the people to realize that the characteristics of children—their sense of wonder, their innocence, their ability to forgive quickly—were characteristics that everyone needed in order to be part of God's kingdom.

Jesus welcomed the children and showed them what God's love was like by touching them and blessing them. As teachers you have the opportunity to show the children you teach what God's love is like. When you are patient, kind, consistent, and respectful with your children, you are modeling God's love.

Jesus loves you, and Jesus loves me.

If time is limited, we recommend those activities that are noted in **boldface**. Depending on your time and the number of children, you may be able to include more activities.

ACTIVITY	TIME	SUPPLIES	
Happy Hearts	**10 minutes**	**Reproducible 8A, crayons or markers, safety scissors, masking tape**	JOIN THE FUN
Stop!	10 minutes	Reproducible 8B	
Sign and Sing	5 minutes	None	BIBLE STORY FUN
Bible Story: Jesus Loves Me	**10 minutes**	**None**	
Bible Verse Fun	**10 minutes**	**Bible**	
Through the Crowd	5 minutes	None	
Wave and Wiggle	5 minutes	scarfs or crepe paper streamers cut into 12-inch lengths	
Guess Who?	5 minutes	happy heart (Reproducible 8A), masking tape	LIVE THE FUN
Beanbag Prayers	**5 minutes**	**beanbag or crumpled paper ball**	

Supplies

Reproducible 8A, crayons or markers, safety scissors, masking tape

Happy Hearts

Photocopy the happy heart **(Reproducible 8A)** for each child. Cut out the hearts. Or let older preschool children cut out the hearts themselves using safety scissors.

Give each child a heart. Read the words printed on the heart as you write the child's name in the space provided. Let the children decorate the hearts with crayons or markers. When each child has finished decorating the heart, use masking tape to attach the heart on a wall or table near your story area.

Say: Today our Bible story is about how Jesus loved the children.

> **Jesus loves you, and Jesus loves me.**

Supplies

Reproducible 8B

Stop!

Photocopy the stop sign **(Reproducible 8B)**. Have the children go to a side of the room opposite from your story area. Make sure the area between that space and the story area is clear of any obstacles.

Say: Today our Bible story is about how Jesus loved the children. Mothers and fathers wanted to bring their children to see Jesus. Some of Jesus' friends did not think Jesus had time for children. But Jesus told his friends to "Let the children come to me." Let's pretend we are little children going to see Jesus. I will tell you how to come to Jesus. *(Show the children the stop sign.)* When you see the stop sign and hear me say, "Stop!" freeze right where you are.

Give the children the first direction and have them move across the room to your story area. After a few minutes hold up the stop sign and shout, "Stop!" Have the children freeze wherever they are. Then give the children the next direction. Continue until the children are in your story area. Have the children sit down.

Hop, little children, hop to see Jesus.
March, little children, march to see Jesus.
Tiptoe, little children, tiptoe to see Jesus.
Crawl, little children, crawl to see Jesus.

Sign and Sing

Supplies

None

Teach the children the chorus to "Jesus Loves Me" using signs from American Sign Language. Sign and sing the song together.

After the children are familiar with the signs, play a game. Sing the song again; sign the word *yes* each time it appears in the chorus, but do not sing it. Sing the song several times. Sign and leave out the next word in the chorus each time you sing until the children are only signing the chorus.

Remind the children that Jesus loves each one of us.

> ### Jesus loves you, and Jesus loves me.

Jesus Loves Me
Jesus loves me! this I know,
For the Bible tells me so.
Little ones to him belong;
They are weak, but he is strong.

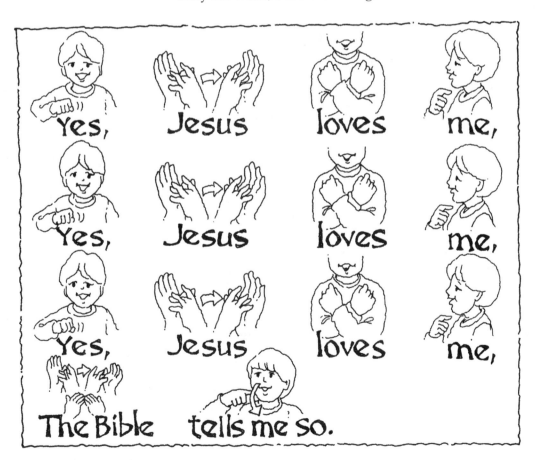

Jesus Loves Me

by Daphna Flegal

Have the children sign and repeat "Yes, Jesus loves me" each time it appears in the story.

"Jesus is here!" said the people in the villages. They hurried to where Jesus was teaching.

"Jesus is here!" said the people in the cities. They hurried to where Jesus was teaching.

"Jesus is here!" said the people from the countryside. They hurried to where Jesus was teaching.

Soon there was a crowd of people listening to Jesus. They wanted to hear what Jesus had to say about God. They all knew that Jesus loved them.

Yes, Jesus loves me! *(Sign the words.)*

"Jesus is here!" said the mothers holding their babies. They hurried to bring their babies to see Jesus.

"Jesus is here!" said the fathers walking with their sons and daughters. They hurried to bring their children to see Jesus.

"Jesus is here!" said the sisters and brothers playing alongside the road. They hurried to to see Jesus.

The people wanted their children to see Jesus. They wanted Jesus to touch their children. They all knew that Jesus loved their children.

Yes, Jesus loves me! *(Sign the words.)*

"Stop!" said a man standing near Jesus. "Do not bring your children to see Jesus."

"Stop!" said a second man. "Jesus does not have time for children."

"Stop!" said a third man. "Take your children home."

The men did not understand that Jesus loved grownups and children. Jesus loved men and women, boys and girls, and even babies.

Yes, Jesus loves me! *(Sign the words.)*

"Wait!" said Jesus. "Let the children come to me."

"Wait!" said Jesus. "Do not send the children away."

"Wait!" said Jesus. "Children belong to God."

Yes, Jesus loves me! *(Sign the words.)*

"Yes!" said the mothers. They brought their babies to Jesus. Jesus touched the babies and blessed them.

"Yes!" said the fathers. They brought their sons and daughters to Jesus. Jesus touched the sons and daughters and blessed them.

"Yes!" said the sisters and brothers. They ran to see Jesus. Jesus touched the sisters and brothers and blessed them.

The babies, the sons and daughters, and the sisters and brothers knew that Jesus loved each one of them.

Yes, Jesus loves me! *(Sign the words.)*

Bible Verse Fun

Choose a child to hold the Bible open to Luke 18:16.

Say: Jesus wanted to see the children, to touch them and bless them. Our Bible verse today tells us what Jesus said.

Say the Bible verse, "Let the children come to me" (Luke 18:16, GNT), for the children. Have the children repeat the Bible verse after you.

Help the children learn the Bible verse by singing. Sing the song printed below to the tune of "London Bridge."

> "Let the children come to me,"
> Come to me, come to me.
> "Let the children come to me;"
> Do not stop them.

Sing the song printed below to the tune of "The Farmer in the Dell." Sing the song several times so that you include each child's name and your own name.

Jesus Loves

> Yes, Jesus loves you and me.
> *(Point to others; point to yourself.)*
> Yes, Jesus loves you and me.
> *(Point to others; point to yourself.)*
> We know Jesus loves us all,
> *(Cross your hands over your heart.)*
> Yes, Jesus loves you and me.
> *(Point to others; point to yourself.)*
>
> Yes, Jesus loves *(child's name)*.
> *(Gently tap the child named on the shoulder.)*
> Yes, Jesus loves *(child's name)*.
> *(Gently tap the child named on the shoulder.)*
> We know Jesus loves us all,
> *(Cross your hands over your heart.)*
> Yes, Jesus loves *(child's name)*.
> *(Gently tap the child named on the shoulder.)*

Jesus loves you, and Jesus loves me.

Supplies

None

Through the Crowd

Choose one child to be the leader. Have the other children line up behind the leader. Instruct the children to stand with their feet apart to make a tunnel.

Say: Let's pretend our line is the crowd of people listening to Jesus. We have to go through the crowd to get close to Jesus.

Begin with the child at the back of the line.

Say: *(Child's name)*, come to see Jesus.

Have the child crawl through the tunnel of legs to the front of the line. Have the child stand up and take his or her place at the front of the line.

Say: *(Child's name)*, Jesus loves you!

Continue until everyone has crawled through the tunnel.

Supplies

scarfs or crepe paper stream- ers cut into 12-inch lengths

Wave and Wiggle

Have the children move to an open area of the room.

Say: Our Bible story today told us that Jesus loved the children. Let's play a game. I will give each of you a scarf or streamer. Hold it, listen carefully, and move as I tell you to move.

Slowly say the following rhyme. Encourage the children to move as di- rected.

This little child waved the scarf down low, Jumped up once, then touched *(her or his)* toes.

This little child waved the scarf in the air, Turned around, then climbed up stairs.

This little child waved the scarf all around, Hopped on one foot, then touched the ground.

This little child waved the scarf up high, Touched the floor, then touched the sky.

These little children were happy, you see, Happy that Jesus loves you and me!

Guess Who?

Have the children sit down in the area where you have taped the happy hearts **(Reproducible 8A)**.

Say: I'm thinking of someone Jesus loves. This someone has ...

Describe one of the children. Say things about the child's hair color, eye color, color of clothing, and so forth until the children guess who the child is. Have the child stand up. Use masking tape to attach a happy heart onto the child's clothing.

Say: Jesus loves *(child's name)*.

Have all the children clap for the child and repeat: **Jesus loves** *(child's name)*.

Continue until you have described every child.

Beanbag Prayers

Have the children sit in a circle. Provide a beanbag or crumple paper into a ball.

Say: In our Bible story today Jesus said, "Let the children come to me" (Luke 18:16,GNT).

> ### Jesus loves you, and Jesus loves me.

Say: Let's thank God for Jesus. Let's thank God for each other.

Call a child by name. Have the child hold his or her arms like a basket. Toss the beanbag in the child's "basket."

Say: Thank you, God, for Jesus. We know Jesus loves *(child's name)*. **Amen.**

ALL–IN–ONE BIBLE FUN

A Boy and His Lunch

Bible Verse

Share what you have.

Hebrews 13:16

Bible Story

John 6:1-14

Once there were more than five thousand people who wanted to be with Jesus. Some were sick and wanted Jesus to heal them. Others wanted to hear Jesus talk about God and God's love.

When evening came, Jesus knew these people were hungry. Jesus asked his disciples to feed everyone, but they didn't know how to do it. "We didn't bring any food," they said, "and we don't have enough money to buy supper for this many people."

Then a little boy in the crowd said, "I have five loaves of bread and two fish. I'll share." But the disciples said, "That's not enough to go around."

Like the disciples, we often view life through the lens of limitations. We look at the great needs in the world and feel inadequate to meet those needs. We focus on what we're lacking. We look at the impossible nature of a situation and say, "I can't do anything to make a difference. I don't have enough to offer."

But God invites us to look at life through a lens of abundance, generosity, and possibility. When we're faced with a difficult situation, we can offer to give and do what we can, regardless of how little it seems.

Our God is a God of miraculous power! God can use our gift, no matter how large or small, to help meet the needs of others.

© 2009 Abingdon Press

We can share with others.

If time is limited, we recommend those activities that are noted in **boldface**. Depending on your time and the number of children, you may be able to include more activities.

ACTIVITY	TIME	SUPPLIES	
String Along	5 minutes	Reproducible 9A, scissors, yarn, tape	JOIN THE FUN
Match It Basket	**10 minutes**	**Reproducible 9B, scissors, crayons**	
Count and Chant	5 minutes	small fish and bread pictures (Reproducible 9B)	BIBLE STORY FUN
Bible Story: Jesus Cares for Hungry People	**10 minutes**	**None**	
Bible Verse Fun	**10 minutes**	**Bible**	
Swish, Swish	10 minutes	Reproducible 9A, scissors, tape	
Share and Tell	5 minutes	None	
Pass the Basket	10 minutes	basket, slice of bread or un-sliced sandwich roll	LIVE THE FUN
Beanbag Prayers	**5 minutes**	**beanbag or crumpled paper ball**	

Supplies

Reproducible 9A, scissors, yarn, tape

String Along

Photocopy and cut out the two fish (**Reproducible 9A**) for each child. Cut yarn into lengths of 2 to 3 yards. Tape one end of a length of yarn onto the nose of each fish. Hide the fish in the room. Weave the length of yarn around the room. Go over and under furniture. Place the loose end of the yarn near your door.

As each child enters, give the child one of the loose ends of yarn. Let the child follow the yarn to find the fish. Have the child put the fish in a basket or box lid in your story area. Let each child find a second fish.

Say: Today our Bible story is about a time when Jesus was teaching many, many people. The people were hungry. They had listened to Jesus talk all day long. Jesus wanted to give the people food to eat. A little boy brought Jesus his lunch to share. The boy had five loaves of bread and two fish. Jesus used the boy's lunch to feed all the people. Jesus cared about people and shared food with them.

> ## We can share with others.

Supplies

Reproducible 9B, scissors, crayons

Match It Basket

Photocopy the basket of bread and fish picture (**Reproducible 9B**) for each child. Cut the small picture strips from the pictures. Cut the small pictures apart.

Give each child a basket and set of small pictures. Encourage the children to match the small pictures of bread and fish to the larger pictures in the basket picture. Help the children notice the spots on one fish and the stripes on another fish. Help the children notice the different line patterns on the loaves of bread.

Say: Today our Bible story is about a time when Jesus was teaching many, many people. The people were hungry. A boy brought Jesus his lunch to share. The boy had two fish and five loaves of bread. Jesus used the boy's lunch to feed all the people. Jesus cared about people and shared food with them. We can share with others.

Let the children use crayons to decorate the basket of fish and bread. Save the small pictures for the "Count and Chant" activity (page 93).

Count and Chant

Tape two of the small fish pictures **(Reproducible 9B)** on two of each child's fingers. Tape the five bread pictures **(Reproducible 9B)** on one of your hands. Say the poem printed below. Hold up the five bread pictures on your hand when you say, "Five loaves of bread." Have the children hold up their fingers with the fish pictures when you say, "and two little fish."

Supplies

small fish and bread pictures (Reproducible 9B)

Five loaves of bread
(Hold up five fingers.)
And two little fish.
(Hold up two fingers.)
My, oh my, what a tasty dish!
(Rub stomach.)

Five thousand people came
From far and near,
To see the man Jesus,
God's son so dear.
They sat on the hillside
And listened all day
To the wonderful things
Jesus had to say.

Five loaves of bread
(Hold up five fingers.)
And two little fish.
(Hold up two fingers.)
My, oh my, what a tasty dish!
(Rub stomach.)

They sat so long,
It began to grow dark.
They became so hungry,
They would eat a shark.
But when Jesus' friends
Took a look around,
A small boy's lunch
Was the food they found.

Five loaves of bread
(Hold up five fingers.)
And two little fish.
(Hold up two fingers.)
My, oh my, what a tasty dish!
(Rub stomach.)

They boy was happy
To share his lunch.
Though he didn't think
It would feed this bunch.
But Jesus took the food
And then calmly said,
"Thank you, God,
For this fish and bread."

Five loaves of bread
(Hold up five fingers.)
And two little fish.
(Hold up two fingers.)
My, oh my, what a tasty dish!
(Rub stomach.)

Five loaves and two fish
Fed everyone there,
And they ate and they ate
Without a care.
They gathered the leftovers—
Twelve baskets when done.
They knew Jesus loved them
Each and everyone.

Five loaves of bread
(Hold up five fingers.)
And two little fish.
(Hold up two fingers.)
My, oh my, what a tasty dish!
(Rub stomach.)

Jesus Cares for Hungry People

by Peg Augustine

Have the children count "one, two, three, four, five thousand people" with you each time it appears in the story. Have the children hold up their fingers as you count together.

Jesus and his friends traveled around the countryside telling people about God and God's love. Sometimes Jesus stopped to help people who were sick. Sometimes he stopped to talk to people who were sad or lonely.

Everyone wanted to get close to Jesus and to listen to him and to talk to him. One day Jesus and his friends got into a boat and started across a lake. Some people who wanted to talk to him saw Jesus in the boat. The people began hurrying around the lake to the other side. They passed other people and told them they were going to see Jesus. Soon there was a large crowd of 5,000 people.

One, two, three, four, five thousand people!
(Hold up fingers as you name each number.)

The people walked so fast, they reached the other side before the boat did. When Jesus saw the crowd of people waiting for him, he smiled at them and walked up the hill.

Jesus sat down on a rock and began to talk. All day the crowd of 5,000 people sat close to him and listened to him.

One, two, three, four, five thousand people!
(Hold up fingers as you name each number.)

Jesus' friends came to Jesus and said, "We've been here all day and soon it will be dark. The people need to eat. We should tell them to go home now."

"No," Jesus said. "We should not send them away hungry. We must feed them."

"But Jesus," Philip said, "we do not have enough money to buy food for them. There must be 5,000 people here."

One, two, three, four, five thousand people!
(Hold up fingers as you name each number.)

"Do we have any food?" Jesus asked.

"There is a boy here who has five small loaves of bread and two fish," Andrew said. "He wants to share his food, but such a little bit will not feed this many people."

One, two, three, four, five thousand people!
(Hold up fingers as you name each number.)

Jesus smiled at the little boy and took the food he wanted to share. He thanked God for the food. Then he began to tear it into smaller pieces. Jesus' friends brought baskets of fish and bread around to the 5,000 people.

One, two, three, four, five thousand people!
(Hold up fingers as you name each number.)

All the people ate until they had enough. The friends went around again and gathered up all that was left. There were still twelve baskets of food!

The people were rested and happy. They knew that Jesus loved them—all 5,000 people.

One, two, three, four, five thousand people!
(Hold up fingers as you name each number.)

Bible Verse Fun

Choose a child to hold the Bible open to Hebrews 13:16.

Say: Today our Bible story is about a time when Jesus was teaching many, many people. Jesus wanted to give the people food to eat. A little boy brought Jesus his lunch to share. Jesus used the boy's lunch to feed all the people. Jesus cared about people and shared food with them.

We can share with others.

Say the Bible verse, "Share what you have" (Hebrews 13:16), for the children. Have the children say the Bible verse after you.

Help the children learn the Bible verse by singing. Sing the song printed below to the tune of "The Wheels on the Bus."

Oh, let's all say our Bible verse,
Bible verse, Bible verse.
Oh, let's all say our Bible verse,
"Share what you have."

Sing the song printed below to the tune of "Are You Sleeping." Sing one phrase and then have the children echo the phrase after you.

The Boy's Lunch

"Feed the people, (Feed the people,")
Jesus said. (Jesus said.)
"They are getting hungry.
(They are getting hungry.)
Give them food. (Give them food.")

"There's no money, (There's no money,")
his friends said. (his friends said.)
"There's too many people,
(There's too many people.)
to buy food. (to buy food.")

"Here is my lunch, (Here is my lunch,")
a boy said. (a boy said.)
"With five loaves and two fish.
(With five loaves and two fish.)
I will share. (I will share.")

Jesus gave thanks, (Jesus gave thanks,)
for the lunch. (for the lunch.)
And because a boy shared,
(And because a boy shared,)
All were fed. (All were fed.)

Supplies

Reproducible 9A, scissors, tape

Swish, Swish

Photocopy and cut apart the fish **(Reproducible 9A)** for each child. Tape one fish for each child on the floor all around the room. Have the children move to an open area of the room. Sing the Bible verse song (page 95) and let the children move as you sing. Stop singing anywhere in the song.

Say: Swish, swish, stand on a fish.

Have the children find a fish picture to stand on. When everyone is standing on a fish, have the children say the Bible verse together: "Share what you have" (Hebrews 13:16). Repeat this part of the game several times.

Remove half the fish taped to the floor. Sing the song again and have the children move around the room. Stop singing.

Say: Swish, swish, share a fish.

Since there are fewer fish than there are children, more than one child will have to stand on each fish.

Say: Jesus cared about hungry people and shared food with them.

> ## We can share with others.

Supplies

None

Share and Tell

Have the children sit down on the floor. Sit in a chair or on the floor a little distance apart from the children.

Say: The boy shared his lunch of two fish and five loaves of bread with Jesus. Jesus cared about hungry people and shared the food with them. Let's think about ways we can share with others.

Call the children one at a time to come and stand next to you.

Say: (Child's name) jump two times and come to me. (clap five times, hop two times, blink five times, pat your knee two times, touch your nose five times)

Encourage the child to name something we can share with others. Help the children think of things such as food, clothing, money, toys, crayons, paper, and so forth.

Pass the Basket

Have the children sit in a circle. Place a slice of bread or an unsliced sandwich roll in a basket.

Say: **The boy shared his lunch of two fish and five loaves of bread with Jesus. Let's share one piece of bread and see how far it will go.**

Invite the children to pass the basket and break off a small piece of bread. Keep passing the basket until the remaining piece of bread is very small.

Say: **Jesus cared about hungry people and shared food with them. We can share with others.**

Let the children eat their pieces of bread.

Say: **Thank you, God, for food to eat. Help us share with others. Amen.**

Beanbag Prayers

Have the children sit in a circle. Provide a beanbag or crumple paper into a ball.

Say: **In our Bible story today a boy shared his lunch with Jesus. Jesus used the boy's lunch to feed many, many people. Jesus cared about hungry people and shared food with them.**

We can share with others.

Say: **Let's thank God for Jesus. Let's thank God for each other.**

Call a child by name. Have the child hold his or her arms like a basket. Toss the beanbag in the child's "basket."

Say: **Thank you, God, for Jesus. We know Jesus loves** (*child's name*). **Amen.**

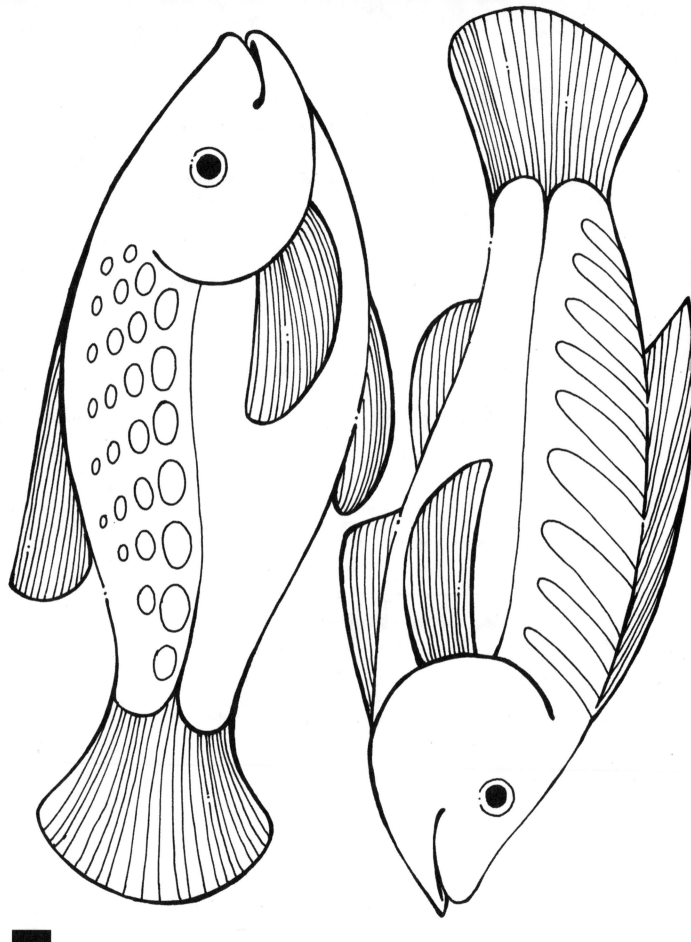

REPRODUCIBLE 9A

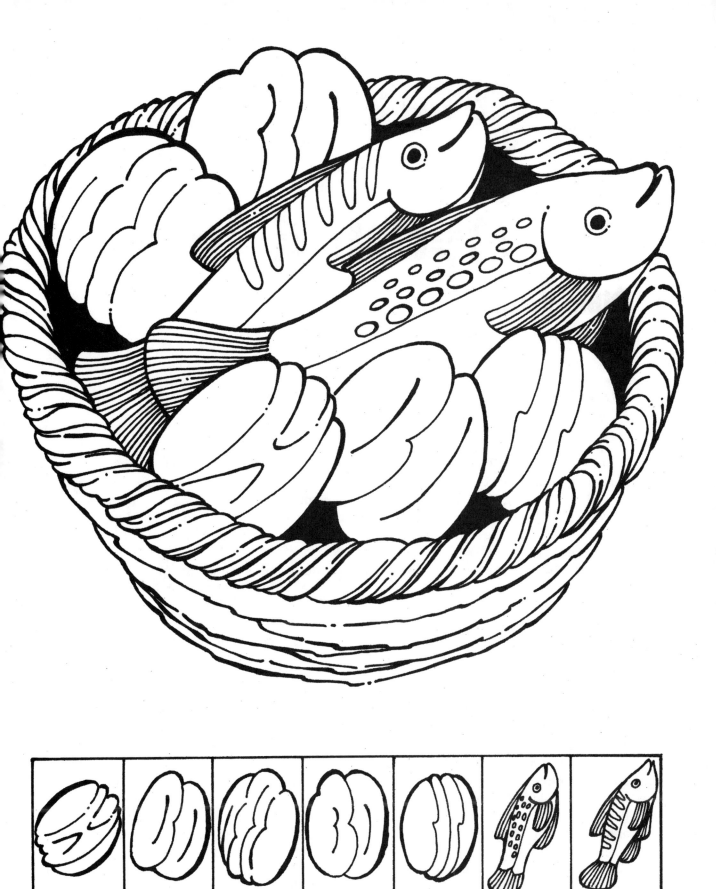

REPRODUCIBLE 9B

All-in-One
BIBLE PRESCHOOL
FUN

Peter and John

Bible Verse

Love is kind.
1 Corinthians 13:4

Bible Story

Acts 3:1-10

Today's story is about Peter and John and the healing of a man who could not walk. Peter and John were going to the Temple to pray. They passed by a man sitting at the gate of the Temple. Because the man could not walk his friends would carry him to the gate so that he could beg for money from people entering the Temple. When he saw Peter and John, he asked them for money. Peter replied, "I have no silver or gold, but what I have I give you; in the name of Jesus Christ of Nazareth, stand up and walk" (Acts 3:6). The man immediately stood up and entered the Temple, leaping and praising God.

This healing miracle took place after Pentecost. It was at Pentecost that Jesus' followers received the gift of the Holy Spirit. The Holy Spirit filled the frightened band of followers who hid after the crucifixion and resurrection with power. They now preached and taught and healed without fear.

Peter and John were two of Jesus' closest followers. The man that Peter and John saw at the gate to the city had been unable to walk since birth. He was not able to work

and had to beg for money to buy food. Instead of money, however, Peter healed the man in the name of Jesus. Peter and John wanted everyone to understand that the man was healed by the power of Jesus.

Young children enjoy helping. Sometimes it is easier to do things yourself, but if a child's offer of help is constantly refused or the work redone, soon the child will quit offering. Accept your children's gifts of help.

When the man was healed, he immediately praised God for his healing. We can help children praise God for God's love and care. Provide opportunities for your children to express their praise to God.

Teacher's Note: There are many movement activities in today's lesson. Be sensitive to children who have physical disabilities. Modify activities or choose alternative activities to fit the needs of your children. Make it clear to the children that God loves all people: those who can run and jump, and those who cannot.

We can help one another.

If time is limited, we recommend those activities that are noted in **boldface**. Depending on your time and the number of children, you may be able to include more activities.

ACTIVITY	TIME	SUPPLIES	
Leaping Feet	15 minutes	**Reproducible 10A, crayons or markers, masking tape, safety scissors**	JOIN THE FUN
Shake a Leg	5 minutes	None	BIBLE STORY FUN
Bible Story: Leap for Joy	**10 minutes**	**J card (Reproducible 10A)**	
Bible Verse Fun	**10 minutes**	**Bible**	
J Is for Jump	10 minutes	Reproducible 10A, paper bag	
Praise God	5 minutes	None	
Heidi Helper	5 minutes	Reproducible 10B, scissors, masking tape	LIVE THE FUN
Flashlight Prayers	**5 minutes**	**flashlight**	

Supplies

Reproducible
10A, crayons
or markers,
masking tape,
safety scissors

Leaping Feet

Photocopy the heart card, J card, and the pair of feet **(Reproducible 10A)**. You will use the J card with the Bible story and the "J Is for Jump" activity (see pages 104 and 106). You will use the heart cards with the "J Is for Jump" activity. You will need a pair of feet for each child. Cut out the feet around the solid oval. Or let older preschool children cut out the feet themselves using safety scissors.

Let the children decorate the feet with crayons or markers. Point out the word *joy* that is printed on the feet.

Say: Today our Bible story is about a man who could not walk. Something happened that had the man jumping for joy. We will find out what happened in our Bible story.

Help the children tape the paper feet to the tops of their shoes. You may want to wrap lengths of masking tape completely around the shoes. Have the children move to an open area of the room.

Say: Let's pretend we have leaping feet. Let me see you jump around the room.

Give the children a few minutes to jump and leap around the room.

Say: Stop!

Lead the children in the following motions. After moving as directed for a few minutes, say stop! and have the children freeze where they are. Give the next direction and encourage the children to move.

**Jump on one foot.
Jump on two feet.
Jump forward three times.
Jump backwards one time.
Jump as high as you can.
Jump one time and then sit down.**

Say: Peter and John were friends of Jesus. They did something to help the man who could not walk that had the man jumping for joy. We will find out what Peter and John did to help the man in our Bible story today.

We can help one another.

Shake a Leg

Have the children sit so that there is room to stretch and move without touching another child.

Say: Let's pretend we cannot move our legs or arms. Stretch out on the floor and be very still.

Pause for a few minutes.

Say: Now let's move each arm and leg.

Lift one arm high in the air.
Shake your hand.
Wiggle your fingers.
Lift your other arm high in the air.
Shake your hand.
Wiggle your fingers.
Shake both hands.
Put your arms down.
Lift one leg high in the air.
Wiggle your foot.
Lift your other leg high in the air.
Wiggle your foot.
Wiggle both feet.
Put your legs back down.

Have the children sit up.

Say: Listen carefully. I will call each one of you by name. When I call your name, stand up and jump to the story area. Then sit down.

Call each child by name. Have the child stand up, jump to your story area, and sit down.

Say: Today our Bible story is about a man who could not walk. Peter and John were friends of Jesus. They did something to help the man who could not walk. After Peter and John helped the man, the man jumped for joy.

We can help one another.

Leap for Joy

by Daphna Flegal

Show the children the J card **(Reproducible 10A)**.

Say: Each time I say the name *Jesus*, I will hold up the J card. J is the first letter in *Jesus*. It is also the first letter in the word *jump*. When I hold up the card, everyone jump up and then sit back down.

Peter and John were friends of **Jesus**. *(Hold up the J card.)* One day Peter and John were going to the Temple. As they walked by the gate of the Temple, they saw a man sitting on a mat.

"Please help me," said the man. "I cannot walk. I cannot work to have money for food. Please give me money so I can buy food to eat."

Peter and John stopped beside the man. They wanted to help him, but they had no money to give to him.

"Look at us," said Peter.

The man looked up. He saw the two friends of **Jesus**. *(Hold up the J card.)*

"I don't have any silver or gold money," said Peter. "But I will give you something in the name of **Jesus**." *(Hold up the J card.)*

Peter took the man's hand. "Stand up and walk!" said Peter.

The man held on tight to Peter's hand. He stood up! The man felt his feet and ankles become strong.

"Praise God," shouted the man. "I can walk!" The man walked into the Temple.

"Praise God," shouted the man. "I can jump!" The man jumped around the Temple.

"Praise God," shouted the man. "I can leap!" The man leaped around the Temple.

The people in the Temple saw the man leaping and jumping and praising God.

"How did this happen?" The people asked. "We know this man could not walk."

Peter spoke to the people in the Temple. He said, "We helped this man walk in the name of **Jesus**." *(Hold up the J card.)*

Bible Verse Fun

Choose a child to hold the Bible open to 1 Corinthians 13:4.

Say: Peter and John were friends of Jesus. They helped the man who could not walk. When they helped the man, they were being kind.

We can help one another.

Say the Bible verse, "Love is kind" (1 Corinthians 13:4), for the children. Have the children repeat the Bible verse after you.

Help the children learn the Bible verse by singing. Sing the words printed below to the tune of "Row, Row, Row Your Boat."

> Love, love, love is kind.
> "Love is kind," you see.
> The Bible tells us "love is kind."
> Now sing again with me.

Sing the song printed below to the tune of "The Wheels on the Bus."

The Man at the Gate

The man at the gate said, "Help me, please." *(Hold out hand.)*
"Help me, please; help me, please."
The man at the gate said, "Help me, please, I cannot walk."

Peter and John said, "We've no gold." *(Shake head no.)*
"We've no gold; we've no gold."
Peter and John said, "We've no gold, But we will help."

"In the name of Jesus, stand up and walk." *(Walk in place.)*
"Up and walk, up and walk."
"In the name of Jesus, stand up and walk, Stand up and walk."

The man at the gate stood up and walked. *(Walk in place.)*
Up and walk, up and walk.
The man at the gate stood up and walked. He was made strong.

The man at the gate jumped up and down, *(Jump in place.)*
Jumped up and down, jumped up and down.
The man at the gate jumped up and down, Shouting God's praise.

© 2001 Abingdon Press

BIBLE STORY FUN

Supplies

Reproducible
10A, paper
bag

J Is for Jump

Photocopy the heart and J card (**Reproducible 10A**). You will need the same number of hearts as there are children and three or four J cards.

Have the children sit in a circle. Show the children one of the hearts.

Say: Peter and John helped the man who could not walk. When they helped the man, Peter and John were being kind. These hearts can remind us of our Bible verse, "Love is kind" (1 Corinthians 13:4). I will put these heart cards in a paper bag. When you reach inside and pick a heart card, say the Bible verse.

Show the children one of the J cards.

Say: When Peter and John helped the man walk again, the man jumped for joy and praised God. The word "jump" begins with the letter "J." I will put these J cards in a paper bag. When you reach inside and pick a J card, shout, "Jump for joy!" When somebody shouts "Jump for joy," everybody stand up and jump up and down.

Place all the cards inside a paper bag. Pass the bag around the circle. As each child takes the bag, have the child reach inside and pull out a card. If the child pulls out a heart, have the child say the Bible verse. If the child pulls out a J card, have the child shout, "Jump for joy!" Each time a child shouts "Jump for joy!" have all the children stand up and jump. Then have the children sit back down and continue passing the bag around the circle.

Supplies

None

Praise God

Ask: How do you think the man felt when Peter and John helped him to walk again?

Say: Or story said he was so happy he jumped for joy and praised God. Let's praise God.

Encourage the children to jump as you say the following chant.

I praise God with my feet.
I praise God with my feet.
I can jump, jump, jump, jump, jump.
I praise God with my feet.

I praise God with my heels.
I praise God with my heels.
I can click, click, click, click, click.
I praise God with my heels.

I praise God with my toes.
I praise God with my toes.
I can tap, tap, tap, tap, tap.
I praise God with my toes.

I praise God with my feet.
I praise God with my feet.
I can jump, jump, jump, jump, jump.
I praise God with my feet.

Heidi Helper

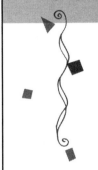

Photocopy the happy face and sad face **(Reproducible 10B)**. Cut out the faces. Use masking tape to attach the two faces on the floor on opposite sides of the room. Make sure the area between the faces is clear of obstacles.

Say: Peter and John helped the man who could not walk. Let's think about some ways we can help one another. I will tell you stories about a make-believe child named Heidi Helper. If Heidi Helper does something to help in the story, go stand by Heidi's Happy Face. If Heidi Helper does not help in the story, go stand by Heidi's Sad Face.

Read one of the short stories printed below. Encourage the children to move to one of the faces after each story.

Father is cooking soup for supper. Heidi Helper puts the bowls, napkins, and spoons on the table.

"Heidi Helper," calls Mother. "Please come to the kitchen and help me empty the trash cans." "No!" shouts Heidi Helper. "I don't want to!"

Heidi Helper's brother falls and scrapes his knee. Heidi Helper holds her brother's hand while Mother puts medicine on the scrape.

Heidi Helper is spending the night with Grandma. When it's time for bed, Heidi Helper leaves her toys all over the floor.

Heidi Helper puts away the crayons when it is cleanup time at day care.

Flashlight Prayers

Have the children sit in a circle. If possible, turn off the lights in your classroom. Shine a flashlight around the circle as you say the first two lines on the following rhyme. Stop the light so it shines on one child. (Be careful not to shine the light in a child's face.) Say the third and fourth lines. Have the child stand up and repeat the Bible verse, "Love is kind" (1 Corinthians 13:4).

> 'Round and 'round goes the light
> 'Til one of our friends it finds.
> *(Child's name)*, now stand up and say,
> "Love is kind."

While the child is still standing, **say: Thank you, God, for** *(child's name)*.

Have the child sit back down in the circle. Continue until every child has a turn.

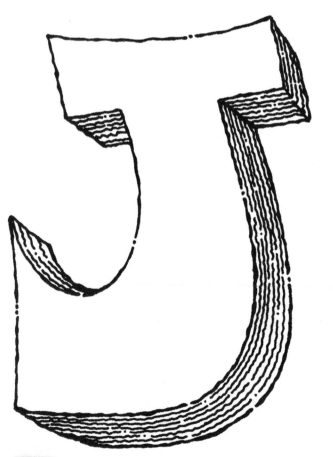

ALL–IN–ONE BIBLE FUN

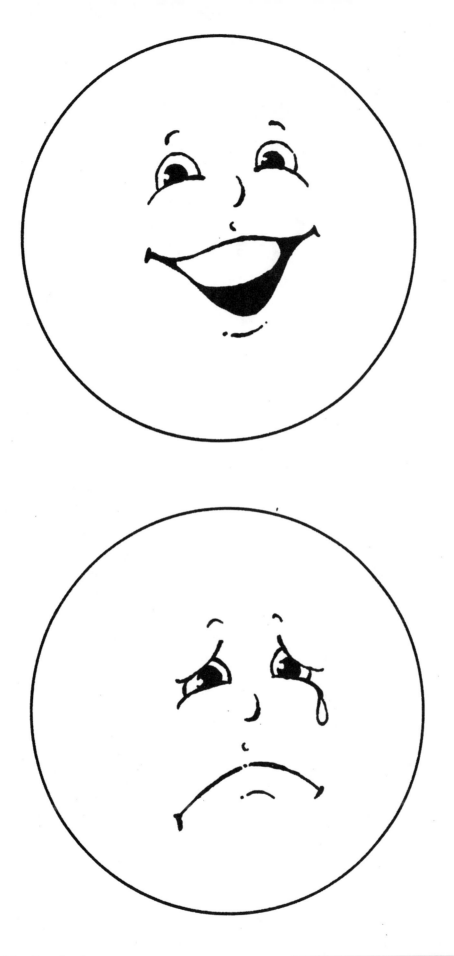

REPRODUCIBLE 10B

Dorcas

Bible Verse

Love is kind.

1 Corinthians 13:4

Bible Story

Acts 9:36-42

Today's Bible story centers around a New Testament woman named Dorcas. Dorcas was a widow who lived in the city of Joppa. "She was devoted to good works and acts of charity" (Acts 9:36). When she became ill and died, the followers of Jesus asked Peter to come to Joppa. Peter came, and Dorcas' friends showed Peter all the clothing Dorcas had made for them. Peter went to Dorcas and raised her from the dead. The news about Dorcas spread throughout Joppa, and many people became Christian as a result of this miracle. Dorcas was also known as Tabitha. She is the only woman in the Book of Acts to be identified as a disciple. "Now in Joppa there was a disciple whose name was Tabitha, which in Greek is Dorcas" (Acts 9:36).

The raising of Dorcas from the dead can lead to many questions for young children. They already have trouble understanding the concept of death. Young children view death as temporary and reversible. Answer the children's questions as honestly as you can. Remember that it is all right to say something like, "I don't know, but I do know that God loves us and always cares for us."

The emphasis for this lesson is on Dorcas' life of service. Dorcas was not a preacher or a teacher or an apostle, but she used the skills she had to the glory of God. She was a seamstress, making clothes for those in need.

Dorcas spent her time helping and giving to others. Young children can learn to freely help others. As a teacher, you can encourage children to make helping a habit by planning classroom routines such as cleanup; by offering opportunities for your children to do things for others; and by affirming children when they offer to help you or others.

We are being kind when we share.

If time is limited, we recommend those activities that are noted in **boldface**. Depending on your time and the number of children, you may be able to include more activities.

ACTIVITY	TIME	SUPPLIES	
Robe-a-Rama	**10 minutes**	**Reproducible 11A, glue, shallow pans, scissors, yarn**	JOIN THE FUN
Tunic Tiptoe	10 minutes	Bible-times costume or shirt, two chairs	
In and Out	10 minutes	Bible-times costume or shirt	BIBLE STORY FUN
Paper Bag Robes	10 minutes	paper grocery-size bags, scissors, crayons or markers	
Bible Story: Dorcas	**10 minutes**	**Reproducible 11A, scissors, tape**	
Bible Verse Fun	**10 minutes**	**Bible, Bible-times costume or shirt**	
Coverup Capers	10 minutes	Reproducibles 11A and 11B, scissors	
Robe Rally Review	5 minutes	Bible-times costume or shirt, chair	LIVE THE FUN
Flashlight Prayers	**5 minutes**	**flashlight**	

Supplies

Reproducible 11A, glue, shallow pans, scissors, yarn

Robe-a-Rama

Photocopy the robe (**Reproducible 11A**) for each child. Cut off the strip of robes from the top of the page. You will need 10 robe squares for each child. Save one robe square to use with the Bible story (page 114) and nine robe squares to use with the "Coverup Capers" activity (page 116).

Let the children decorate the robes by gluing on pieces of yarn. Cut the yarn into six-inch lengths. Pour glue into shallow pans. Show the children how to run the lengths of yarn through the glue and then place the yarn on their paper robes. Set the paper robes aside to dry.

Say: Today our story is about a woman named Dorcas. Dorcas was a follower of Jesus. She sewed robes and clothing for people in need. She knew that followers of Jesus were kind to others. When she shared her robes, Dorcas was being kind.

> ## We are being kind when we share,

Supplies

Bible-times costume or shirt, two chairs

Tunic Tiptoe

Say: Today our story is about a woman named Dorcas. Dorcas was a follower of Jesus. She sewed robes and clothing for people in need. She knew that followers of Jesus were kind to others. When she shared her robes, Dorcas was being kind.

Show the children the costume or shirt.

Say: Let's pretend this costume (or shirt) is one of the robes Dorcas made.

Place the costume or shirt over a chair on one side of the room. Place another chair on the opposite side of the room. Have the children line up behind the chair with the costume or shirt.

Choose a child to begin. Have the child put on the costume or shirt (unbuttoned), tiptoe to the chair across the room, and then tiptoe back to the line. Have the child take off the costume or shirt and give it to the next child in line. Have the next child put on the costume or shirt and tiptoe to the chair and back to the line. Continue until each child has a turn.

In and Out

Supplies

Bible-times costume or shirt

Say: Today our story is about a woman named Dorcas. Dorcas made clothes for people in need. She knew that followers of Jesus were kind to others. When she shared her robes, Dorcas was being kind.

> ### We are being kind when we share.

When Dorcas sewed, she would have pushed a needle in and out of the cloth to stitch the clothes together. *(Hold the costume or shirt. Pantomime pushing a needle in and out of the cloth.)* **Let's pretend that we are Dorcas' needle going in and out of the cloth.**

Move the children to an open area of the room. Have the children stand side by side and hold hands. Spread the children out so that they are standing with their arms outstretched and held up while they hold hands.

Choose the child at the beginning of the line to begin. This child will be Dorcas' needle. Have the needle weave in and out underneath the children's hands. When the needle comes to the end of the line, have the needle join hands with the line. The child now at the beginning of the line becomes the next needle. Practice until the children understand the movement. Sing the following verse to the tune of "The Farmer in the Dell." Have the needle move in and out of the other children. Continue until each child has a turn.

> The needle goes in and out,
> The needle goes in and out.
> Sewing robes for those in need,
> The needle goes in and out.

Paper Bag Robes

Supplies

paper grocery-size bags, scissors, crayons or markers

Cut a grocery-sized paper bag to make a Bible-times robe for each child. Turn each sack upside down. Cut a slit up the middle of one of the wider sides. At the top of the side, continue to cut and form a circular shape for the child's neck. In each of the two narrower sides, cut a hole large enough for the child's arm to go through. If the bags have printing on them, turn the bags inside out.

Give each child a paper robe. Let the children decorate the robes with crayons or markers. Encourage the children to wear their robes.

Dorcas

by Daphna Flegal

Photocopy the picture story. Or write the story on a large piece of paper. Mount the paper on a wall or spread it on the floor. Leave spaces as indicated in the story. Give each child a robe square **(Reproducible 11A)**. *Place a loop of tape on the back of each square. Tell the children the story. Each time you come to a space, choose a child to tape a robe square in the space. At the end of the story have any child who has not already taped on a robe square add a square. Count the robe squares with the children.*

Dorcas was a follower of Jesus. Dorcas liked to sew. She made

for people who needed clothes to wear. She liked to share with others.

Dorcas became sick and died. All her friends were sad. They asked Peter

to come. They showed Peter the   Dorcas had made.

Peter went to Dorcas. He said a prayer. Then he said, "Dorcas, get up."

Dorcas got up. She was alive! Everyone was amazed. Many people be-

lieved in Jesus because of Dorcas.

Dorcas continued to make   for people in need. She made

many   .

ALL–IN–ONE BIBLE FUN

Bible Verse Fun

Choose a child to hold the Bible open to 1 Corinthians 13:4.

Say: Dorcas was a follower of Jesus. She sewed robes and clothing for people in need. She knew that followers of Jesus were kind to others. When she shared her robes, Dorcas was being kind.

We are being kind when we share.

Say the Bible verse, "Love is kind" (1 Corinthians 13:4), for the children. Have the children repeat the Bible verse after you.

Help the children learn the Bible verse by singing. Sing the words printed below to the tune of "Row, Row, Row Your Boat."

> Love, love, love is kind.
> "Love is kind," you see.
> The Bible tells us "love is kind."
> Now sing again with me.

Hold the costume or shirt in your hands. Pretend to sew the costume. As you are pretending to sew, teach the children the song "Robes and Coats." It is sung to the tune of "Hot Cross Buns." Encourage the children to pretend to sew as they sing.

Robes and Coats

> Robes and coats,
> Robes and coats,
> Dorcas helped when she sewed
> Robes and coats.

BIBLE STORY FUN

Supplies

Reproducibles 11A and 11B, scissors

Coverup Capers

Photocopy the game card page **(Reproducible 11B)** for each child. Use the robe strips you cut from the robe picture **(Reproducible 11A)**. Each child will need nine robes. Cut apart the robes. Give each child the game card and nine robes.

Say: Dorcas was a follower of Jesus. She sewed robes and clothing for people in need. Dorcas knew that followers of Jesus shared with others. When she shared her robes, Dorcas was being kind.

> ### We are being kind when we share.

Say: Let's play a game. I will say the name of something we can share. Look on your card to find a picture of the thing I name. Cover up the picture with one of the paper robe squares. When all your squares are covered, stand up and shout, "Love is kind!"

Say the name of one of the items pictured on the game card. Help the children know which picture to cover up. Talk with the children about how we share the item named.

Clothes — We can bring the clothes we have outgrown to share with other children whose families don't have enough money to buy clothes.

Food — We can bring cans of food to share with people who need food to eat. If your church has a food pantry, tell the children about the pantry.

Money — We can bring our offering to church. One way our church uses the money is to help people in need.

Toys — We can share toys with our friends.

Crayons —We can share crayons with our friends.

Kind words — We can say kind things to each other. Can you think of some kind words?

Love — We can share love with one another.

Bible — When we tell our friends and family Bible stories, we are sharing the Bible.

Jesus — When we tell our friends and family about Jesus, we are sharing the good news about Jesus.

When all the pictures are covered, have all the children stand up and shout, "Love is kind!"

116

Robe Rally Review

Supplies

Bible-times costume or shirt, chair

Have the children sit in a circle. Place a chair in the center and cover it with a Bible-times costume or shirt.

Begin with the child on your left or to your right and give the instructions below. When the child reaches the chair, have the child say the Bible verse and then crawl back to his or her spot in the circle. Change the directions for each child and use any statement about Dorcas.

Continue this activity until all the children have had a chance to say the Bible verse.

If you remember Dorcas followed Jesus, crawl to the robe.
If you remember Dorcas made many robes, hop to the robe.
If you remember Dorcas shared with others, walk to the robe.
If you remember Dorcas was kind, tiptoe to the robe.

Flashlight Prayers

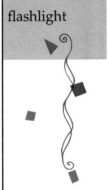

Supplies

flashlight

Have the children sit in a circle. If possible, turn off the lights in your classroom. Shine a flashlight around the circle as you say the first two lines on the following rhyme. Stop the light so it shines on one child. (Be careful not to shine the light in a child's face.) Say the third and fourth lines. Have the child stand up and repeat the Bible verse, "Love is kind" (1 Corinthians 13:4).

> **'Round and 'round goes the light**
> **'Til one of our friends it finds.**
> ***(Child's name)*, now stand up and say,**
> **"Love is kind."**

While the child is still standing, **say:** *(Child's name)* **is a follower of Jesus. Thank you, God, for** *(child's name)*.

Have the child sit back down in the circle. Continue until every child has a turn.

We are being kind when we share.

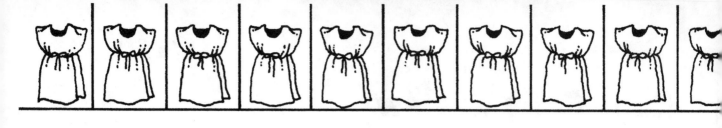

REPRODUCIBLE 11A

ALL–IN–ONE BIBLE FUN

REPRODUCIBLE 11B

119

All-in-One
BIBLE PRESCHOOL
FUN

Paul

Bible Verse

Love is kind.

1 Corinthians 13:4

Bible Story

Acts 9:1-9

Saul, more commonly known by his Greek name, Paul, became an important missionary for Jesus. Paul was actively working against the early followers of Jesus. He thought that the people who followed Jesus were teaching against the laws of God. Saul was a Roman citizen from an influential family, and he had the power to persecute the people of the early church. Saul stood and watched as Stephen, a young Christian who preached about Jesus, was stoned to death. Saul began searching people's houses to find followers of Jesus to drag them off to prison.

In today's Bible story Saul was traveling along the road to the city of Damascus. He was looking for followers of Jesus to bring back to Jerusalem to stand trial. Suddenly a bright light flashed around Saul. He fell to the ground and heard a voice saying, "Saul, Saul, why do you persecute me?" (Acts 9:4). The voice was the voice of Jesus. Jesus told Saul to go to Damascus and wait to be told what to do. Saul got up and realized he was blind.

The Lord told a follower of Jesus named Ananias to go to Saul and help Saul regain his sight. Ananias did not want to go to Saul, because he knew how Saul was persecuting followers of Jesus. Ananias did as the Lord directed, however, and went to Saul. Ananias laid his hands on Saul, and Saul's sight was restored. Saul was baptized and became a follower of Jesus. His teachings and writings helped spread the good news about Jesus to both Jews and Gentiles. Paul's ministry lasted about 30 years and ended with his execution around A.D. 60.

When Paul became a follower of Jesus, his life was dramatically changed. He turned from a life of hatred to a life of love. Help the children you teach learn that they can be followers of Jesus and show love to others.

Teacher's Note: We will use only the name Paul in today's lesson. Switching back and forth from Saul to Paul may be confusing for young children. The Hebrew name Saul is the same as the Greek name Paul.

We can be followers of Jesus.

If time is limited, we recommend those activities that are noted in **boldface**. Depending on your time and the number of children, you may be able to include more activities.

ACTIVITY	TIME	SUPPLIES	
Chat About Change	**10 minutes**	**Reproducible 12A, scissors**	JOIN THE FUN
Change It!	10 minutes	Reproducible 12A, scissors, tape	
Flashlight Frolics	10 minutes	flashlight	BIBLE STORY FUN
Shine and Sign	5 minutes	flashlight	
Bible Story: A Change for Paul	**10 minutes**	**None**	
Bible Verse Fun	**10 minutes**	**Bible**	
On the Road With Paul	5 minutes	None	
Paul's Little Instruction Book	15 minutes	Reproducible 12B, safety scissors, crayons or markers, stapler and staples or paper punch, yarn	
Kind Followers	5 minutes	None	LIVE THE FUN
Flashlight Prayers	**5 minutes**	**flashlight**	

Supplies

Reproducible 12A, scissors

Chat About Change

Photocopy the change cards **(Reproducible 12A)**. Cut the cards apart along the solid lines. Make several sets of cards for this activity. You will also need change cards for the "Change It!"activity if you choose to include it. Mix the cards and spread them out on a table or rug.

Say: **These cards show things that change. Match the pictures to see the changes.**

The matches are caterpillar to butterfly, tadpole to frog, acorn to oak tree, and egg to bird.

Say: **Today our Bible story is about a man named Paul. Paul did not like followers of Jesus. Then something happened to Paul. Paul saw a very bright light. After Paul saw the light, he made a change. He became a follower of Jesus.**

> ## We can be followers of Jesus.

Supplies

Reproducible 12A, scissors, tape

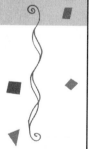

Change It!

Photocopy the change cards **(Reproducible 12A)** so that you have enough cards for at least two of the children to have the same card. Tape the cards to the children's clothing. Make sure each child knows the card that is taped to his or her clothing. Have the children stand in a circle.

Say: **When I call out frog, everyone who has a frog picture changes places. When I call out butterfly, everyone who has a butterfly picture changes places. Stay in the circle. When I say, "Everybody, change it!" everyone in the circle will change places with someone else.**

Practice to be sure the children understand the game. Call out one of the things pictured on the cards, like caterpillar. Have all the children wearing a caterpillar card change places in the circle. Play the game until everyone's card has been named at least once. Occasionally say, "Everybody, change it!"

Say: **Today our Bible story is about a man named Paul. Paul made a change. He became a follower of Jesus. We can become followers of Jesus.**

Flashlight Frolics

Supplies

flashlight

If possible, turn off your classroom lights. Shine the flashlight on the floor. Say the following rhyme and shine the flashlight to a spot somewhere in your room. Choose spots that the children can safely move to.

> Follow the light around the floor,
> Under the table or near the door.
> Follow the light wherever it shines,
> Then remember—love is kind.

Repeat the rhyme several times, shining the light on a different area of the room each time. When you are ready to stop the game, shine the light on your story area. Have the children move to the story area and sit down.

Say: **Today our Bible story is about a man named Paul. Paul did not like followers of Jesus. Then something happened to Paul. Paul saw a very bright light. After Paul saw the light, he made a change. He became a follower of Jesus.**

We can be followers of Jesus.

Shine and Sign

Supplies

flashlight

Teach the children the Bible verse, "Love is kind" (1 Corinthians 13:4), using signs from American Sign Language. Once the children are familiar with the signs, have the children put their hands in their laps. Shine the flashlight on one child's hands. Have that child sign the Bible verse while the light is shining on him or her. Give each child a turn.

Love   Kind

Art: Robert S. Jones

A Change for Paul

by Daphna Flegal

Have the children sign (page 123) and say the Bible verse, "Love is kind" (1 Corinthians 13:4), each time it appears in the story.

"All the followers of Jesus should be put in jail," said Paul angrily.

Paul was not a follower of Jesus. He did not know that:

Love is kind. *(Sign and repeat.)*

"I'm going to stop the followers of Jesus from telling others about Jesus," Paul said. "I'm going to go to another city to look for followers of Jesus."

Paul was not a follower of Jesus. He did not know that:

Love is kind. *(Sign and repeat.)*

Paul started down the road. Suddenly Paul saw a very bright light. Paul was so surprised, he fell to the ground.

"Paul, Paul," said a voice from the light. "Why are you unkind to people who follow me?"

"Who are you?" asked Paul.

"I am Jesus," said the voice. "Go to the city. I will send someone to teach you what I want you to do."

Paul listened to Jesus. He was learning that:

Love is kind. *(Sign and repeat.)*

Paul stood up. He could not see anything. Some of his friends led him to the city. Paul stayed in the city three days.

A man named Ananias came to help Paul. "Paul, Jesus wants me to teach you how to be a follower of Jesus," said Ananias. He helped Paul see again.

Ananias helped Paul become a follower of Jesus. Paul learned that:

Love is kind. *(Sign and repeat.)*

Paul made a change. He became a follower of Jesus. He told many, many people the good news about Jesus. Paul wrote letters that told people about Jesus' love.

Paul was a follower of Jesus. Paul knew that:

Love is kind. *(Sign and repeat.)*

Bible Verse Fun

Choose a child to hold the Bible open to 1 Corinthians 13:4.

Say: Paul did not like the followers of Jesus. Then Paul made a change. He became a follower of Jesus.

We can be followers of Jesus.

Say: When Paul changed to be a follower of Jesus, he learned that Jesus wanted him to be kind to others.

Say the Bible verse, "Love is kind" (1 Corinthians 13:4), for the children. Have the children repeat the Bible verse after you.

Help the children learn the Bible verse by singing. Sing the words printed below to the tune of "Row, Row, Row Your Boat."

> Love, love, love is kind.
> "Love is kind," you see.
> The Bible tells us "love is kind."
> Now sing again with me.

Have the children stand in a circle. Walk around the circle as you sing the first stanza of the song "Paul Became a Follower" to the tune of "Do You Know the Muffin Man?" Walk around the circle in the opposite direction as you sing the second stanza.

Paul Became a Follower

> Paul became a follower,
> a follower, a follower.
> Paul became a follower
> of Jesus, our friend.
>
> I can be a follower,
> a follower, a follower.
> I can be a follower
> of Jesus, our friend.

© 1996 Cokesbury

On the Road With Paul

Have the children pretend to travel on the road with Paul. Let the children walk in place and pretend to see things on the way. Use the following narration as a guide.

Let's pretend we are traveling with Paul. Let's walk. (*Walk.*) **We are going to the city to find the followers of Jesus. We do not like the followers of Jesus.** (*Stomp.*) **Suddenly we see a bright light.** (*Stop.*) **The light is so bright we can't see.** (*Cover eyes.*) **We fall to the ground.** (*Uncover eyes; sit or kneel on the floor.*) **We hear a voice.** (*Cup hands around ears.*) **The voice says, "Paul, Paul, I am Jesus. Why are you being unkind to my followers? Get up, and I will tell you what to do."** (*Get up.*) **Paul still could not see.** (*Cover eyes.*) **Paul's friends led him to the city.** (*Uncover eyes; walk.*) **In the city Paul learned to be a follower of Jesus. He learned that love is kind.** (*Put hands over heart.*)

Paul's Little Instruction Book

Photocopy the "Paul's Little Instruction Book" pages **(Reproducible 12B)** for each child. Cut the pages apart along the solid lines. Older preschool children may cut the pages apart themselves using safety scissors.

Give each child a cover of the book. Let the children decorate the covers with crayons or markers.

Say: Our Bible story today was about a man named Paul. Paul did not like the followers of Jesus. But when Paul saw the bright light and heard the voice of Jesus, he made a change. He became a follower of Jesus.

Give the children the two Bible verse pages. Let the children decorate these pages with crayons or markers.

Say: When Paul became a follower of Jesus, he learned what Jesus wanted him to do. We can find some of the things Paul learned in our Bible. Paul learned that love is kind. He learned that love never ends.

Have the children repeat the Bible verses. Give the children the last page. Write the children's names in the spaces provided. Let the children decorate the pages with crayons or markers.

Say: Paul became a follower of Jesus. We can be followers of Jesus.

Help each child put the pages of the instruction book together as the pages are numbered. Staple the lefthand edge of the pages together. Or use a paper punch to make two holes in the lefthand edge of the pages. Tie a piece of yarn through the holes to make the book. Read the book to the children.

Kind Followers

Say: Paul did not like the followers of Jesus. But when Paul saw the bright light and heard the voice of Jesus, he made a change. He became a follower of Jesus.

We can be followers of Jesus.

Say: Followers of Jesus know that love is kind. I wonder what followers of Jesus do to show others that love is kind.

Ask: Do followers of Jesus listen to stories from the Bible? If they do, say "love is kind!" *(Children repeat "love is kind.")*

Ask: Do followers of Jesus sing songs to praise God? If they do, sing "love is kind!" *(Children sing the words "love is kind.")*

Ask: Do followers of Jesus share food with people who need food to eat? If they do, shout "love is kind!" *(Children shout "love is kind.")*

Ask: Do followers of Jesus pray for one another? If they do, whisper "love is kind!" *(Children whisper "love is kind.")*

Flashlight Prayers

Have the children sit in a circle. If possible, turn off the lights in your classroom. Shine a flashlight around the circle as you say the first two lines on the following rhyme. Stop the light so it shines on one child. (Be careful not to shine the light in a child's face.) Say the third and fourth lines. Have the child stand up and repeat the Bible verse, "Love is kind" (1 Corinthians 13:4).

'Round and 'round goes the light
'Til one of our friends it finds.
(Child's name), now stand up and say,
"Love is kind."

While the child is still standing, **say:** *(Child's name)* **is a follower of Jesus. Thank you, God, for** *(child's name).*

Have the child sit back down in the circle. Continue until every child has a turn.

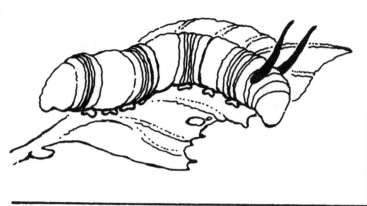

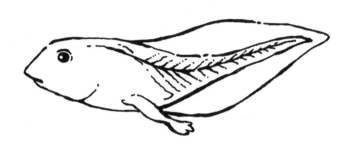

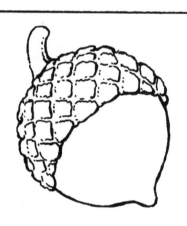

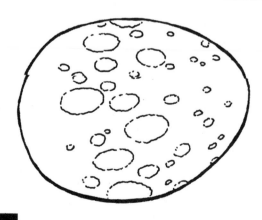

REPRODUCIBLE 12A

1 Corinthians 13:8

Love never ends.

1 Corinthians 13:4

Love is kind,

Name

Paul's Little
Instruction Book

All-in-One
BIBLE PRESCHOOL
FUN

Lydia

Bible Verse

Love is kind.
1 Corinthians 13:4

Bible Story

Acts 16:11-15

Paul and his friends traveled to Philippi, a Roman city in Macedonia. On the Sabbath day Paul went out of the city by the river to a place of prayer. Some women who worshiped God were gathered there. Paul told the women about Jesus. One of the women was named Lydia. Lydia became a follower of Jesus. She and her whole household were baptized by Paul in the river. After the baptism she invited Paul and his friends to stay at her home.

The place of prayer where the women came to worship God was outside the city, because it was against the law to worship God in Phillipi. Paul sought out the place of prayer to begin his preaching and teaching in this Roman city. This company of women was Paul's first congregation in Philippi.

Lydia was probably a wealthy woman. She sold purple cloth, and only the wealthy could afford purple cloth. The dye to make purple cloth came from the secretions of

mollusks. Only a small amount of dye could be made from each shell, so purple cloth was expensive.

Lydia's hospitality was important to the spread of the gospel in Philippi. Her house probably became the base for preaching and teaching in the city of Philippi.

As a teacher you are the Paul for the children you teach. Your commitment can help your children learn about Jesus.

We can learn about Jesus.

If time is limited, we recommend those activities that are noted in **boldface**. Depending on your time and the number of children, you may be able to include more activities.

ACTIVITY	TIME	SUPPLIES	
Color Purple	**10 minutes**	**Reproducibles 13A and 13B, scissors, purple crayons, tape**	JOIN THE FUN
Hop, Hop, Purple, Hop	10 minutes	purple squares and hearts from the "Color Purple" activity (Reproducible 13A), tape	
Purple Walk Around	5 minutes	purple construction paper	BIBLE STORY FUN
Bible Story: Lydia	**10 minutes**	**Reproducible 13B; block, plastic bottle, or paper towel tube; purple construction paper**	
Bible Verse Fun	**10 minutes**	**Bible**	
Where Is Lydia?	10 minutes	purple squares from "Color Purple" activity (Reproducible 13A), glue, clear tape	
Learning With Lydia	10 minutes	Optional: purple cloth	LIVE THE FUN
Flashlight Prayers	**5 minutes**	**flashlight**	

JOIN THE FUN

Color Purple

Photocopy the square, heart pictures, and Lydia face (**Reproducible 13A**). Copy enough so that each child has one square, one heart picture, and one Lydia face. Cut apart the squares, heart blocks, and faces along the solid lines. Give each child one square and one heart block. Save the Lydia faces for later in the lesson. Make one copy of the Lydia figure (**Reproducible 13B**). Cut out the figure.

Say: **Today our Bible story is about a woman named Lydia. Lydia sold purple cloth. Lydia learned about Jesus.**

> ## We can learn about Jesus.

Say: **Since Lydia sold purple cloth, let's color with purple crayons.**

Give each child a purple crayon. Or let the children search through your crayon supply to find all the purple crayons.

Show the children the Lydia figure. Let the children work together to color the figure's robe with purple crayons. Set the Lydia figure aside to use during the Bible story.

Give each child the square and the heart block. Let the children color the squares and hearts with purple crayons. As the children finish coloring, tape the purple squares and hearts all around the room.

Hop, Hop, Purple, Hop

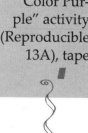

Have the children join you in the center of the room.

Say: **Today our Bible story is about a woman named Lydia. Lydia sold purple cloth. Lydia learned about Jesus. We have taped several purple squares and hearts around our room. When I say, "Hop, hop, purple, hop," I want you to hop to a purple square. When I say the name "Jesus," hop to a purple heart.**

Say, "Hop, hop, purple, hop," and have the children hop to any of the purple squares taped around the room. Say the phrase again and have the children hop to a different square. Occasionally say the name Jesus and have the children hop to any of the purple hearts. When you are ready to stop the game, have the children stay wherever they are in the room.

Purple Walk Around

Supplies

purple construction paper

Place a piece of purple construction paper on the floor.

Say: Hop, hop, purple, hop. Everyone hop to the purple paper.

Have the children hop to the purple paper and sit down around it.

Say: Today our Bible story is about a woman named Lydia. Lydia sold purple cloth. She learned about Jesus.

We can learn about Jesus.

Have the children stand up in a circle around the purple paper. Sing the song "Here We Go Walking" to the tune of "The Wheels on the Bus." Have the children walk around in a circle while you sing.

Here We Go Walking
Here we go walking 'round and 'round,
(Walk in a circle.)
'Round and 'round,
'Round and 'round.
Here we go walking 'round and 'round,
Now let's all sit down.
(Sit down.)

Lydia learned about Jesus,
(Clap hands.)
About Jesus,
About Jesus.
Lydia learned about Jesus.
We can, too.
(Point to self.)

Here we go walking 'round and 'round,
(Walk in a circle.)
'Round and 'round,
'Round and 'round.
Here we go walking 'round and 'round,
Now let's all sit down.
(Sit down.)

Lydia

by Daphna Flegal

*Tape the Lydia figure (**Reproducible 13B**) to a block, plastic bottle, or paper towel tube. Set the Lydia figure in the center of a piece of purple construction paper. Have the children follow the instructions in the story.*

Say: Today our Bible story is about a woman named Lydia. Lydia sold purple cloth. She learned about Jesus.

Lydia sold purple cloth. Touch the purple paper. *(Have the children touch the purple construction paper.)* Lydia liked the color purple. It was a special color. Only people who were rich could afford to buy purple cloth. Lydia was a rich and important person in the city of Philippi.

Lydia loved God. She prayed to God every day. Fold your hands as if you are saying a prayer. *(Have the children fold their hands in prayer.)* Lydia knew some other women who also loved God so Lydia and her friends met outside the city beside the river. There was a law that said you could not pray to God in the city.. The women would sit beside the river to pray to God.

One day Lydia and her friends were sitting beside the river when a man named Paul came over to them. He told them all about Jesus. Lydia listened very carefully. *(Cup your hand around one ear.)* Show me how you listen carefully. *(Have the children cup a hand around one ear.)*

Lydia was happy to learn about Jesus. Show me how you look when you are happy.

(Have the children make a happy face.) Paul baptized Lydia in the river, and she became a follower of Jesus. Lydia wanted her whole family to learn about Jesus. She invited Paul to stay at her house. Paul told Lydia's family about Jesus. Everyone at Lydia's house became a follower of Jesus.

Lydia still sold purple cloth. Touch the purple paper again. *(Have the children touch the purple paper.)* But now Lydia also helped others learn about Jesus.

Bible Verse Fun

Choose a child to hold the Bible open to 1 Corinthians 13:4.

Say: Lydia learned about Jesus from a man named Paul.

We can learn about Jesus.

When Paul told people about Jesus, one of the things he said was that love is kind.

Say the Bible verse, "Love is kind" (1 Corinthians 13:4), for the children. Have the children repeat the Bible verse after you.

Help the children learn the Bible verse by singing. Sing the words printed below to the tune of "Row, Row, Row Your Boat."

> Love, love, love is kind.
> "Love is kind," you see.
> The Bible tells us "love is kind."
> Now sing again with me.

Sing the song "Lydia" to the tune of "Do You Know the Muffin Man?"

Lydia

Lydia sold purple cloth,
Purple cloth, purple cloth.
Lydia sold purple cloth,
Down in the town.

Lydia would pray to God,
Pray to God, pray to God.
Lydia would pray to God,
Outside the town.

Lydia met Paul one day,
Paul one day, Paul one day.
Lydia met Paul one day.
Down by the river.

He told her about God's Son,
About God's Son, about God's Son.
He told her about God's Son,
Jesus, our friend.

She became a follower,
A follower, a follower.
She became a follower
Of Jesus, our friend.

© 2001 Abingdon Press.

Supplies

purple squares from "Color Purple" activity (Reproducible 13A), glue, clear tape

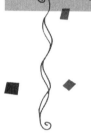

Where Is Lydia?

Have each child go around the room and untape one of the purple squares from the "Color Purple" activity (**Reproducible 13A**). Give each child a Lydia face (**Reproducible 13A**).

Say: Today our Bible story is about a woman named Lydia. Lydia learned about Jesus.

We can learn about Jesus.

Let the children glue the faces over the black dot printed in the center along one edge of the square. Help the children roll the square into a tube. Tape the edges together. Show the children how to put the tube over their fingers to make Lydia finger puppets.

Say the following finger play for the children. Have the children start with the Lydia puppets behind their backs. Have the children bring the Lydia puppets to the front each time you say, "Here I am."

Lydia, Lydia, Where Are You?

(Start with the Lydia puppet behind your back.)
Lydia, Lydia, where are you?
Where are you today?
Here I am by the riverside,
(Bring the Lydia puppet in front.)
I've come to see friends and pray.

(Put the Lydia puppet behind your back.)
Lydia, Lydia, where are you?
Where are you today?
Here I am by the riverside,
(Bring the Lydia puppet in front.)
Listening to what Paul has to say.

(Put the Lydia puppet behind your back.)
Lydia, Lydia, where are you?
Where are you today?
Here I am by the riverside,
(Bring the Lydia puppet in front.)
I learned about Jesus today.

Learning With Lydia

Say: We can learn about Jesus.

Have the children repeat the following list of things we can learn about Jesus. Hold up a finger for each thing.

1. Christmas is Jesus' birthday.
2. Jesus is God's son.
3. Jesus loved the children.
4. Jesus loves me and everyone.
5. Jesus is my friend.

Say: Lydia learned about Jesus. Let's pretend to be Lydia and think about what we have learned about Jesus.

Choose a child to stand up in front of the other children. Optional: Wrap a purple cloth over the child's head or shoulders.

Ask: Lydia, Lydia dressed in purple, what have you learned about Jesus?

Have the child say something about Jesus. Give suggestions from the list. Continue until every child has a turn to be Lydia. Expect that the children may say the same thing each time.

Supplies

Optional: purple cloth

Flashlight Prayers

Have the children sit in a circle. If possible, turn off the lights in your classroom. Shine a flashlight around the circle as you say the first two lines on the following rhyme. Stop the light so it shines on one child. (Be careful not to shine the light in a child's face.) Say the third and fourth lines. Have the child stand up and repeat the Bible verse, "Love is kind" (1 Corinthians 13:4).

> **'Round and 'round goes the light**
> **'Til one of our friends it finds.**
> *(Child's name)*, **now stand up and say,**
> **"Love is kind."**

While the child is still standing, **say:** *(Child's name)* **is a follower of Jesus. Thank you, God, for** *(child's name)*.

Have the child sit back down in the circle. Continue until every child has a turn.

Supplies

flashlight

REPRODUCIBLE 13A

All-in-One BIBLE FUN

Are you

- Feeling the budget pinch in your children's ministry?
- Unsure of the number of children you'll have in Sunday school each week?
- Working with a Sunday school program that doesn't meet each week?

LET THE FUN BEGIN

Order Today!

Preschool

Elementary

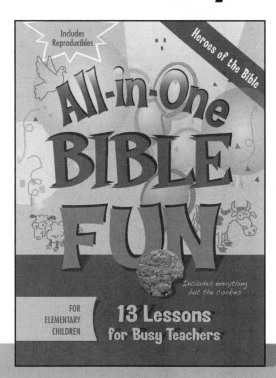

All-in-One Bible Fun

is available for preschool- and elementary-age children. Each book will focus on a specific theme:

- *Stories of Jesus*
- *Favorite Bible Stories*
- *Fruit of the Spirit*
- *Heroes of the Bible*

- Thirteen complete lessons in each book

- No additional components to purchase

- Each book includes lesson plans with your choice of arrival activities, a Bible story, a Bible verse and prayer, and games and crafts

- Material is undated so teachers can use the books throughout the year

All-in-One Bible Fun: 13 Lessons for Busy Teachers

Stories of Jesus—Preschool 978-1-426-70778-0
Stories of Jesus—Elementary 978-1-426-70779-7

Favorite Bible Stories—Preschool 978-1-426-70783-4
Favorite Bible Stories—Elementary 978-1-426-70780-3

Fruit of the Spirit—Preschool 978-1-426-70785-8
Fruit of the Spirit—Elementary 978-1-426-70782-7

Heroes of the Bible—Preschool 978-1-426-70784-1
Heroes of the Bible—Elementary 978-1-426-70781-0

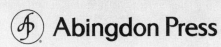

Abingdon Press

abingdonpress.com | 800-251-3320

One Room SUNDAY SCHOOL®

Working with a broader age group?

One Room Sunday School is designed specifically for a program where four or more age groups are taught in one classroom.

For children age 3 through middle school!

Students will grow together through comprehensive Bible study, application of Bible lessons to everyday discipleship, and a variety of age-appropriate activities.

 Abingdon Press

Live B.I.G.'s
One Big Room

A Proven Sunday School Program for Mixed-Age Group Children's Ministries

kit includes everything you need for the quarter

- 3 DVDs
- One Music CD
- One Leader Book

For children age 3 through middle school!

Abingdon Press